# HEAPING COALS

# HEAPING COALS

## From Media Firebrand
## to Anglican Priest

# MICHAEL COREN

DUNDURN
PRESS

Publisher: Meghan Macdonald | Acquiring editor: Kwame Scott Fraser | Editor: Russell Smith
Cover designer: Laura Boyle
Cover image: James Stikeman

**Library and Archives Canada Cataloguing in Publication**

Title: Heaping coals : from media firebrand to Anglican priest / Michael Coren.
Names: Coren, Michael, author.
Identifiers: Canadiana (print) 20240341112 | Canadiana (ebook) 20240341120 | ISBN 9781459752597 (softcover) | ISBN 9781459752610 (EPUB) | ISBN 9781459752603 (PDF)
Subjects: LCSH: Coren, Michael. | LCSH: Anglican Church of Canada—Clergy—Biography. | LCSH: Journalists—Canada—Biography. | LCGFT: Autobiographies.
Classification: LCC BX5620.C667 A3 2024 | DDC 283.092—dc23

We acknowledge the support of the Canada Council for the Arts and the Ontario Arts Council for our publishing program. We also acknowledge the financial support of the Government of Ontario, through the Ontario Book Publishing Tax Credit and Ontario Creates, and the Government of Canada.

Dundurn Press
1382 Queen Street East
Toronto, Ontario, Canada M4L 1C9
dundurn.com, @dundurnpress

*To Elizabeth, an inspiration.*

# INTRODUCTION

I grew up in what was known as a mixed family. Makes the whole thing sound almost culinary. Having said that, food did always play a significant role in my upbringing: bland, often unhealthy, but always plentiful. My parents came from fairly poor backgrounds and were determined that their children would always be surrounded by food. Steak and fries, bacon and eggs, sausage rolls, seemingly endless bars of chocolate, and cookies of every variety in every place. Even now, I struggle with my cholesterol.

Dad was Jewish, and Mum partly. As a child, I lived in Ilford in Essex, an area with a significant Jewish population — perhaps 15 percent — but had very few Jewish friends and seldom encountered anybody who really cared about the whole thing. In other words, anti-Semitism did exist but was rare.

One incident, however, does stick in the mind and in the gut.

I was seven years old. In those seemingly innocent and safe days, the local children would spend most of their summer holidays at what was known as "the rec" — the recreation ground a few streets away from where I lived. It's odd to remember all this now, because I would never have let my children go to a park on their own, without any supervision. Different days, I suppose; different levels of confidence, different fears. Once we were there, huge and spontaneous games of soccer would develop, and we'd run miles as we played. Then we'd eat chocolate and candy we'd bought from local shops — Mars, KitKat, Cadbury's Flake, Sherbet Fountains, and other names and products that no longer exist but still spark in me all sorts of delightful memories. Then we'd walk or, more likely, cycle home, because bicycles were ubiquitous. The calories consumed and then burned off must have been astronomical, but calories weren't counted or considered, by us or by our parents. We'd also make instant friends, and on one of these dreamy, insouciant days, I began chatting to a boy who didn't go to my school. We laughed, kicked a ball around, and did what kids did. He asked if I wanted to go back to his house for an orange drink and a cookie. I agreed. We sat on the floor in his front room, indulging in perfect childish, spotless joy.

Then his dad came home. It was as if darkness had entered the room in a man-shaped cloud: he seemed immediately angry and unhappy. There were loud voices, punchy demands, and then the boy said to me, with tears in his eyes and in obvious fear, that I had to leave. The whole thing bewildered me, but hey ho, kids' television started at 4 p.m., so I didn't really care. It was strange and unusual but nothing more.

It was only later, strangely but perhaps typically, that I realized what the father was saying. "Who is he? Is he a fucking Jew? He is, isn't he? Get him out of here!" He'd shouted it, repeated it, and I now think that he may have been drunk. I don't think the boy knew what a Jew was. Not sure I did either, really. I suppose I should have explained my background and then said, "I'm only half-Jewish. Could I at least stay for lunch?" But I was a child. And the father was a rotting, repugnant, hateful, bullying old Nazi. I've no idea how he knew about my background. Perhaps it was just a lucky fascist guess.

I told nobody — not because I thought it wise or unwise, but because I didn't really think about it at all. There was too much goodness and light in my life for a slither of grime to make much of a difference. If I'd let my father know what had happened, he might have taken a slightly muscular approach to the situation: he'd boxed for the Royal Air Force and had grown up dealing with people very much like the one I'd just met. But I didn't tell him. I just moved on with being a child. A happy, half-Jewish child.

Twenty years later, I was sitting in one of the departure lounges at Heathrow Airport, only looking up from my book to see if my flight had been announced. Suddenly, someone was standing over me.

"It's Michael, isn't it?" a tall, good-looking man asked.

I said it was.

"I'm sure you don't remember me," he continued, "but years ago you came to my house and my dad ordered you to leave."

A pause, and then hidden or buried emotions came to the surface, and a nasty experience that had been folded away somewhere suddenly came back, eerily and bewilderingly familiar. Yes, I did remember. I did remember.

"I've often thought of trying to contact you, to reach out," he said, blushing slightly, and a little hesitant. "That day, I didn't really know what was going on, but I knew later, when my dad tried to involve me in his fascist politics. He was a hard-core Holocaust denier and racist." He stopped, and I thought he was going to cry. He steadied himself, and then said, "I now know that it was why my mum drank so much and why eventually she left him. Left us. He died a deeply unhappy and lonely man, and it's taken me a lot of years to forgive him for what he did, what he said, what he was, and what he tried to do to me and turn me into."

Then another pause, and this time the tears were obvious.

I stood up, put my hand on his arm, and explained that I'd never blamed him, and that at the time I hadn't even realized what was being said.

"I know," he replied. "It was all confusion for me as well. Child abuse, really. I think he hated people, most people, because at some level he hated himself."

We sat down in a more private area, and this son of a ghost told me that back then, he hardly knew what Jewish was or what it meant. We laughed.

"I know now, though." He grinned. "I married a beautiful, clever, kind woman. A Jewish woman. And while she didn't care what religion I was, I converted to Judaism because I wanted to share with her — be more like her, I suppose. Meaning I do know what a Jew is now."

At which point we both laughed, then cried a little, and then hugged. Then we had the meal we should have had so many years earlier. So, yes, I did stay for lunch this time.

# CHAPTER ONE

## ESSEX BOY

I was born on January 15, 1959, in Thorpe Coombe Hospital in Walthamstow, on the edge of London, where the great city meets the often-mocked county of Essex. The county is rural as well as urban, but the parts of it that join London are thought to contain loud young women, aggressive young men, working-class caricatures, and gauche new money. It's largely a snobbish condescension, and Essex isn't very different from most other places in this regard. As a maternity hospital, Thorpe Coombe had seventy beds, and my mother remembered that they gave her Guinness to drink because, they said, it was good for Mum and for baby. The hospital closed in 1973 and would later become a mental health facility. I wonder if Guinness was still being recommended.

My parents were then living in a small, rented apartment in Leytonstone, a few miles away. No central heating, a bath once a week, but it all seemed warm and safe and fine to me. I've thought hard about first memories; I'm pretty sure the earliest is of Mum peeling vegetables in the small kitchen, and the smell of the nearby oil heater. Even now, anything even close to that is comforting. My grandparents, Mum's parents, lived in the same building. Dave and Bertha Schneider were very "East End." They were raised and lived in Whitechapel, infamous for Jack the Ripper, famous for being the home of waves of immigrants from first France (Huguenot refugees fleeing persecution), then Irish Catholics, then eastern European Jews, now Muslims from Bangladesh. Poor, rough, close-knit.

Very close-knit for some of the locals, because Bertha became pregnant with my Uncle Maurice in 1928, two months before she and Dave got married. They lived on the same street. Dave was an orphan, raised by a Jewish family (presumably his birth mother was Jewish, too), and Bertha a blond, blue-eyed Anglican. They were a handsome couple who would live and love together for many decades, never leaving the small, basic apartment and hardly ever apart, other than for the few years that Dave was in North Africa, Sicily, and Italy during the Second World War. "Every time I saw him, he had another stripe on his arm," my mum would say.

Many years later, I hired a genealogist to trace my maternal grandmother's family tree, and a large binder was presented to me that would, I was told, explain everything. In truth, family histories do and they don't. Grandma had been Bertha Jones, and the book traced her particular branch of the Jones family — and her mother's family, the Cranmers — back to the mid-eighteenth century. Almost all of them had been farm labourers in rural Essex, owning no property and obviously struggling to make a living. Eventually the clan left what now seems like bucolic rural England for urban and noisy east London. By the late nineteenth century, they simply couldn't manage financially to continue farming at their basic level, and London offered work and money. To me it seems a shame; to them it seemed unavoidable.

Phil and Sheila Coren on their wedding day. A handsome couple.

My mother, Sheila, was raised in Whitechapel and then nearby Stepney Green. She spent all her early life in the East End of London, apart from a year in Walsham le Willows in rural Suffolk. During the Second World War, the Luftwaffe's Blitz was screaming its way through the country, and many of the children of London and other major cities were evacuated to safer spots. Around 3.5 million young people would eventually be housed temporarily outside of the most bombed areas. The policy was voluntary, sensible, and humane, but not according to young Sheila, who hated every moment of being away from her home. I drove her back to visit Walsham many years later, and it was beautiful. "Not when I was bloody there," said Mum. It was, of course, but it wasn't home. She felt like a foreigner.

Dad — Philip Coren — was raised in a small apartment in Hackney, just to the north of where Mum was from. It was also a poor area, and home to a large Jewish community. The area wasn't as communal and co-existing as the East End, and there was more anti-Semitism and friction. Dad was one of four children — two boys, two girls — and unlike my mum, he was raised in a relatively orthodox Jewish home. His mother, Grandma Rose, was born in Europe, and there was still something strongly eastern European about the home. As a child, I'd visit with my parents and always felt somehow out of place there. Where Mum's parents were loving and fun, I found Dad's to be more distant and controlling.

So, three of my grandparents were Jewish. Judaism, as opposed to Jewishness, runs through the maternal line, and although I'm more than Jewish enough for anti-Semites, I'm not Jewish enough for some Jews. And even their definition varies, depending on the person and the situation. In Israel, only one Jewish grandparent is required for citizenship under the Law of Return, meaning that there are Israelis who are only tentatively Jewish. There are, for example, Russian-born Israelis who have citizenship but still consider themselves to be of the Russian Orthodox faith. I wonder how that makes Palestinians feel, when their families have been resident for generations? Actually, I don't wonder at all. There are entire books, shelves of them, written about and around this subject, and I've met too many Palestinians to not understand the bitter dilemma. For me, what I was mattered and didn't matter to varying degrees, depending on the situation and the context.

Having a foot in both camps, being a relative outsider — neither one thing nor another, perhaps never quite fitting in — has been a constant theme in my life. Whether it's race, religion, class, or politics, I've seldom been anchored. That's been a comfort and a help, and an ache and a wound. I was sent to Hebrew school when I was a child, but always complained that I had to go and insisted that I didn't want a bar mitzvah — for which I hardly even qualified. My father eventually agreed, which was quite a compromise for someone raised as he was. But then his upbringing wasn't always happy. I discovered later that his father, Harry Coren, had hit his children, and I get the impression that my dad was the usual target. Rose, my grandma, was gentler and more loving, but life couldn't have been easy for my dad. He never once raised his hands to me, but he had a temper, he shouted, he could be triggered by something so small, and that pushed me away. I now believe that the shouting and the impatience were likely the result of the way he'd been treated as a child. It's impossible to understand that when you're also a child, though, and it made life much more challenging. Dad was generous, incredibly hard-working, and good in so many ways, but the bloody temper was like a huge splinter that would never disappear. My mum gave as good as she got, however, and their arguments were loud and frequent. I loved them, they loved me, but that constant possibility of screaming and shouting was painful and destabilizing.

Sometimes I'd be left in the care of my great-auntie, who was like a grandma to me. She was from what is now Ukraine but was the Soviet Union when she was a child. We called her "Bubba." She smiled all the time but spoke very little English. While our linguistic communication was limited — her first languages were Yiddish and Russian — our common conversation was love. I could feel it in the way she laughed with me, played with me, sat with me.

Sometimes I'd catch her looking in my direction; staring, really. Even then, long before I could read a proper book or understand the proper world, I could tell that behind the smiles, there was something deeper, perhaps sadder, at work. She always wore dresses that covered the entirety of her arms, but as she was a lady of a former time, this seemed unsurprising. Then, one hot July day, she absent-mindedly rolled up her sleeves and I noticed something.

"What's that, Bubba?" I asked excitedly.

It was the only time she ever seemed upset, even angry with me. She replied that it was nothing, pulled down her sleeves, and turned away.

I thought I'd hurt her somehow, and I might even have had tears in my eyes. All I remember was that she immediately lifted me up and hugged me tighter than ever, in an embrace that seemed like protection and grace knitted together. It wasn't until long after she died, and I was a teenager, that I was finally told Bubba's story. She had been in a death camp, and the mark on her arm was a tattoo. The Nazis sadistically scraped them into the arms of their chosen victims to dehumanize them before torturing and murdering them. She survived, but many of her family and friends did not. I can only imagine the mingling of emotions that was her relationship with me: lamentation for those years spent in hell, for lost loved ones, for slaughtered children. How I wish I could speak to her now; how I wish I could speak to so many of them now.

While most of my father's family had left Poland, Ukraine, and Russia for Britain around 1900, during yet another wave of pogroms, some remained behind. That was my great-aunt's part of the clan. Her brother had fought in the Red Army through most of the Second World War. I met him only once, when I was a child, and he seemed very old. He wore his uniform for the reunion; his medals chimed like a victory march. He drank vodka all day long. He pinched my cheek a lot, and it hurt. "There are two types of vodka," he told me in broken English. "Good vodka … and very good vodka."

Because he spoke Yiddish as well as Russian, during the war he was used as an interpreter. Yiddish is its own language but its basic grammar and vocabulary, although written in the Hebrew alphabet, is Germanic. When German soldiers were interrogated, their lives were often in his hands. He was reluctant to say much about his experiences, but he must have seen such a lot. He was a captain when he left the army, even made a temporary major, and fought all the way through to Germany.

He did tell me one story, about a teenager he and his men captured in 1945. The boy admitted to my uncle that he was in the SS. He cried and he begged. My uncle's commander asked what the boy was saying. "He's a kid who has been digging tunnels for them," my uncle replied. "He's nothing." They let him live. I asked why he had done that, especially when the Nazis had murdered so many of his relatives. With his perennial wide grin briefly gone, he replied, "I'd seen enough of that shit. Sometimes we have to forgive — sometimes we have to forgive."

Less hair now but the gap-tooth is still with me.

I wasn't an only child. My sister, Stephanie, six years older than me, was protective of her little brother. Our relationship has vacillated over the years, and for that I'll always be sorry. We were close as children but drifted apart a little over time. She's a wonderful person, a devoted mother of two girls, and someone I wish I'd been closer to. I think the division was partly a result of family tensions, but in all honesty I'm not entirely sure why it happened. Do any of us really know why arguments start, and what they were about? Sometimes it is for good reason, and the spark is concrete and even sinister, but not in our case. I've never fully understood it, and while I'm reluctant to blame my parents, I do think that sides were taken in arguments, and that we children were exposed to tensions beyond our grasp and understanding. I'm in Canada now, have been for thirty-six years, and Steph is still in England. We chat, we care for one another, but distance and history make anything closer than that very difficult. It's one of the many regrets in my life.

Dad drove a London cab. Lots of Jewish men drove cabs after the Second World War because no family connections were needed, anti-Semitism wasn't an obstacle, and with hard work (fifty-hour weeks and very few holidays), there was a fairly good living to be made. He generally enjoyed and was proud of what he did, but the work was hard and demanding. He kept a diary, and an autograph book. Working in central London for forty years meant that a surprisingly large number of famous people got into his cab. Laurence Olivier ("very nice but very tired"), Alan Alda of *M*A*S*H* fame ("lovely man but wouldn't stop talking"), the actor Richard Harris ("very down to earth, funny, and seemed genuinely curious about what driving a cab was like"). Dustin Hoffman had an artificial fart balloon with him, which he insisted on showing off. Sir Ralph Richardson and Sir John Gielgud, two icons of British theatre, didn't say much but were polite; Peter O'Toole "filled the whole bloody cab with his personality. I liked him."

Jimmy Savile was a famous TV personality in Britain who was beloved for his extensive work for charity. For decades he was one of the most recognizable people in the country; he was given knighthoods by the queen and the pope. After his death, however, he was exposed as a long-term sex abuser and pedophile, a repugnant and sinister man who caused untold harm and damage. Dad had him as a passenger more than once and said, "There's something I don't trust about him — he's not what he seems." Oddly enough, in 1985 at a Roman Catholic Church in central London, the priest asked me to receive the offering — to take a canvas bag around the small congregation to collect donations. Sitting behind a pillar, largely hidden from everybody else, was Jimmy Savile. I've sometimes wondered what was going on in his mind and in his heart. He had groomed and abused up to a thousand children in TV studios and hospitals, and performed sex acts on corpses, yet here he was at a midday mass. It couldn't have been a cover or a way to boost his reputation — there were far larger ceremonies he could have attended, and he'd positioned himself where even the small group of people present that day wouldn't have seen him. Was it guilt, shame; part of a genuine struggle against the hideous nature of his secret and grotesque life?

Dad once had Nobel Prize–winning author Harold Pinter as a passenger, and that was more than a little awkward. Dad had been two years above Pinter at the Hackney Jewish Youth Club, and they'd grown up in similar circumstances. "Good Lord," said Pinter when he got into the cab. "Hello, Philip." My dad was "Phil" to everybody. Harold spoke with a refined, educated English accent; my dad, from an identical background, sounded as you'd expect a working-class Jewish cabbie from Hackney to. Clearly, one of them had worked at it.

How well-known, even famous people behaved in the cab, and how they treated the driver, had a strange effect on my life as a child. These people were on television or in the news, and I'd see them through the lens of my father's experience. If they were rude or dismissive, I'd hear about it vicariously. I grew up disliking world champion racing driver Graham Hill, even though I'd never met him. "Bloody cheap sod" was my dad's biographical analysis. Apparently, he hadn't given a tip at the end of a long trip. Poor man probably just forgot, but Phil Coren didn't.

Dad was highly intelligent; had he been born two decades later, he would likely have gone to university just as his son did, as well as the children of so many people from first- and second-generation immigrant families. He read whenever he could — which wasn't that often — as did my mum, but he worked so very hard that when he got home, he'd watch some television, have his dinner, and fall asleep shortly after going to bed. University was never even a possibility. "I drive this cab," he'd say to me, "so you won't have to." It was said with love and concern, not warning or threat.

He never owned a new car, but when I was thirteen years old, he bought a used one. Up until then he'd used the cab for family trips, and I realized only later how this must have felt. All week long he was an employee, paid by people to drive them around. Now here he was with his wife and children, but to everybody else it would seem as if Phil Coren was still the cabbie, driving where his customers told him to. It meant that the car, old and dented though it was, symbolized a certain dignity and liberation for him.

Mum had been a hairdresser when she lived in the East End, but mostly stayed at home once her children came along. Because of Dad's long hours — and, frankly, his temper — I became much closer to my mother. And she indulged me. Not financially as such, because we weren't at all wealthy, but emotionally and also with respect to my behaviour. It was out of love, but Mum let me do pretty much what I wanted, and that brought out the worst in me. I was a child, and children shouldn't be judged through the prism of adulthood, but my personality was such that Mum's approach empowered a certain selfishness. It was my fault, not hers, but when I look back at the way I sometimes behaved, I cringe. When someone is spoiled, they believe their own self-perception because there are too few boundaries and consequences: relatively harmless for a small child but potentially dangerous for a teenager. I could be a bully, I could be cynical, I could be arrogant. I wasn't brave or adventurous enough to be especially bad, but when I see how well my children behave and how selfless and genuinely good they are, I die a little inside. For what it's worth, I've tried to make amends, to be a different person, and I ask for forgiveness almost every day of my life.

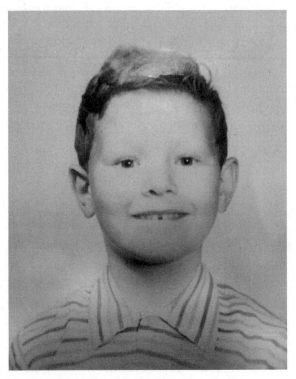

A happy seven-year-old. The shirt was rather cool.

When I was five years old, I went to my first school, Redbridge Primary. The building was a five-minute walk from Highcliffe Gardens in Redbridge, Essex, where we had moved a year earlier. It was more Greater London than rural Essex, and part of what is better known as Ilford. We'd gone from a small apartment to a three-bedroom, semi-detached house, and back then that meant something to people from my family's background. I'll never forget the day my father paid off the thirty-year mortgage and took actual ownership of the house. Back then I didn't quite understand his sense of pride in what he'd achieved, but he was close to the age I am now, and as I write this, I feel tears in my eyes. How I wish I could have shown more appreciation and empathy.

To a large degree, my childhood was safe and secure. I never risked going hungry, I wasn't beaten or abused, and I never thought my parents would get divorced — largely because that was something working-class people hardly ever did back then. But there was the shouting and the arguing, and I do wonder if they would have stayed together if they'd been of another generation or a different social background. I've a feeling they would have separated, or at least gone for some form of professional help, which may well have helped all of us. There was love — real love — but clouded by so much conflict.

But together they did stay, and they made their home in this east London suburb that holds mostly positive memories. The closest underground station was a fifteen-minute walk, and then it was a thirty-five-minute train ride into the centre of London. Yet trips "into town" weren't common when I was small, and always seemed adventurous and eventful. In the summer holidays, Mum would take me to Leytonstone, just a brief bus ride away, to see her parents. They lived in the same apartment block where I had spent the first few years of my life with my parents, and they would spend the rest of their long lives there. Mum visited each Wednesday, so when I was around, I went with her. I remember tea with lots of sugar, thick sandwiches with ham and Spam covered with tomato ketchup, the sound of nearby trains, and the smell of that oil heater again. They didn't have much, never owned but always rented their state-owned home, and seemed so much happier than my father's parents. They were nothing special to most people but everything special to me. Grandma was glamorous, confident, and bold. Grandpa — Dave Schneider — was patient, strong, and kind. He liked his whisky, a habit he'd picked up during the war and which he seemed to pass down to his grandson, and at Christmas time, after he'd had a drink or two, I'd always hear him humming or singing the same tune.

I didn't know at the time what the song was, but my mother told me later that it was a hymn called "Abide with Me." Nothing odd about that, I suppose, other than it wasn't a Christmas song and also that Grandpa was Jewish. Intensely secular, cynical about all religion, but still Jewish. It was only after his death that I discovered what all of this was about. Grandpa had spent almost four years in the British Army during the Second World War, rising up the ranks until he was a senior sergeant. Most of the men in his original unit were dead by 1944. During one of the last engagements in which he took part, Dave and his men were sitting waiting for the shooting, the anger, and the pain to begin, when one of them, a nineteen-year-old Welsh infantryman, began to sing. Many of the other soldiers joined in. Then the singing stopped and the combat began, and by the end of the fight, some of them were dead, including that young Welshman. The song he had been singing was "Abide with Me," and the battle took place at Christmas. Grandpa Dave never forgot, and out of tribute, sorrow, or something beyond my understanding, he kept that fallen warrior's memory alive each year. Grandpa is gone now but I still feel his presence, and I, too, still sing that song to myself.

Abide with me; fast falls the eventide
The darkness deepens; Lord, with me abide.
When other helpers fail and comforts flee,
Help of the helpless, O abide with me.

For some reason, it wasn't one of the hymns we sang at school, but there were certainly morning assemblies where we'd sing traditional Christian songs, and I got to know and love them. The school wasn't Church of England as such but there was an assumed Anglican culture to the place. Most Roman Catholic children generally went to their own school, so those at Redbridge were obviously from fairly secular families. A small but still significant number of Jewish children attended, and one or two were excused from the religious part of assembly if their parents had requested it. I don't recall anybody commenting on this and certainly not objecting in any way. There was one assembly when Gideon Bibles were handed out and the parents of one boy did complain. Thing is, I'd no idea who Gideon was or why any of this mattered, and I'm pretty sure I wasn't alone.

Nostalgia isn't a particular friend to a memoir, but I look back at most of my time at school, between the ages of five and eleven, as largely enjoyable and painless and often rather beautiful. There I first heard of the writings of C.S. Lewis, whose work later became a major influence on my life and beliefs. Miss Power, whose voice seemed like that of an angel, read us *The Lion, the Witch and the Wardrobe*, and I sat on the floor, cross-legged, in sublime captivation. I suppose I was in love with Miss Power, and certainly in love with Lewis's writing. I'd later become friends with Walter Hooper, Lewis's friend and secretary in the last few months of the author's life. I'd see Walter whenever I was in Oxford, and always admired how he was so self-effacing when people came from all over the world to visit him, always wanting to meet not him but to know C.S. Lewis through him. Walter is gone now, and I miss him.

I've always thought that the seeds of my later Christianity were planted when I listened to the words of one of the greatest Christian apologists in recent history. Those words were subtle and implicit, and I'd no idea that I was hearing anything more than an exquisite story that pulled me from reality into the clouds of unknowing, but then that likely made it all the more effective. It was a very different experience from talking to those people I've met over the years who were raised as Christians and then left the faith as soon as they could.

Miss Power read the Lewis book to us in the weeks leading up to Christmas, which was the highlight of all our lives. It still is mine, if I'm honest — the time I briefly return to my childhood. Back then, in the Coren home, a plastic tree would be brought down from the attic and set up in the front room. It was medium sized, with tinsel-wrapped branches that unfolded. We'd hang ornaments all over them. No crosses, no Jesus, no crèche, no Virgin Mary. That would have been inconceivable to my parents. As a family, we weren't opposed to Christianity in any way; we just didn't know very much about it beyond the various Jesus movies. In those, he did seem very cool.

The only reference to Advent was via *Blue Peter*, a television show that probably every child in the country watched. The presenters had an Advent crown, on which a new candle would be lit each week. I didn't know what was going on, but I know I liked it. For me, the Advent crown was about waiting for gifts rather than waiting for the birth of the Messiah.

I remember a small choir from the Salvation Army coming to our door one Christmas and singing carols. Suddenly they stopped, and we heard a man explaining to his uniformed friends that it might be rude to sing about Jesus outside a house where, as he had noticed from the mezuzah, a Jewish family lived. A mezuzah is a piece of parchment inscribed with verses from the Torah, inside a small container, and Jewish people affix it to their door frames. The man put it so delicately and sensitively. This wasn't political correctness but Christian charity. My dad ran to the door, asked them to please continue singing, and then put as much money as he could into their collection tin.

Yet my parents would no more have gone to church than to a synagogue, unless it was for a wedding or a funeral. However, Dad never worked on Yom Kippur, the Day of Atonement. He was a London cab driver when around one-third of all the black cabs in the city were driven by Jewish men. If non-Jewish cabbies had seen him working on that holiest of days, they would have been shocked and told their Jewish friends when they returned to work — not out of malice but surprise. Actually, it was a good day for the non-Jewish drivers because there was so much work around. Dad did work on the Sabbath, Saturdays — when he wasn't at Tottenham, watching the soccer team he had followed since he was tiny; he had lived a few minutes away from their home ground.

The other day he didn't work was Christmas Day, not for religious reasons but because he wanted to spend it with his family. So, Phil Coren worked until 2 a.m. on Christmas Eve to try to make up for the money he would lose by not working the following day. It wasn't because he was mean with money — far from it — but because he supported a family of four on his single income. It has always stung me that I didn't grasp the reality of it all. I would wake up at seven in the morning on Christmas Day, see the sack of presents at the end of my bed, and rush to my parents' bedroom, screaming, "He's been, he's been!" I could never understand why my dad seemed so tired, so lacking in interest. The poor man had had five hours of sleep after a sixteen-hour working day to be able to buy what "he" who had "been" had left me. I know that children aren't supposed to comprehend the struggles of their parents, but even so.

Christmas Day was *Frosty the Snowman* and *Rudolph the Red-Nosed Reindeer* on television, and movies about Allied soldiers escaping from prisoner-of-war camps run by cruel but cartoonish German guards. The Christmas spirit in abundance! I loved the carols, I loved the sense of goodwill to all, I loved the vague ideas I had of the Christmas story, of magic made flesh. The Christian essence was there in an unformed, embryonic way, but there was obviously no established pattern of belief. That would come much later.

As well as Christmas, there was Guy Fawkes Night, on November fifth. Not a religious holiday, not a holiday at all, but a time for celebration.

The date was, of course, the commemoration of the capture and brutal execution in 1605 of a group of Roman Catholic plotters intent on murdering the royal family, the government, and the religious, political, and social establishment in a terrorist atrocity that would have been worse than 9/11. But for me as a child, it was about slightly dangerous fun — slightly dangerous because someone, somewhere would always be hurt by a firework or a flame from a bonfire. The nights became darker earlier, there was mystery and the smell of gunpowder in the air, and we'd eat sausages and drink hot chocolate.

Many years later, on one of my annual visits to London, I was walking back to where I always stay in a Westminster church, just a few minutes from the House of Parliament. I'm a history nerd so know all the places where various events occurred. As I was walking past the precise spot where Guy Fawkes was hung, drawn, and quartered, an American couple stopped me and asked whether anything significant had happened close by. I said yes, lots, then told them the story of Fawkes, with some of the bloody detail about disembowelment, castration, beheading, and limbs sliced off and paraded in different parts of the country.

"My golly!" exclaimed the husband, with his wife looking on anxiously. "Was this recently?"

□

As my time at Redbridge School came to an end, I took what was known as the eleven-plus exam. I passed, though narrowly, I think. Those who failed the examination were sent to secondary modern schools, and those who passed it went to grammar schools. It was streaming, it was selection, it was probably unfair, but it provided a first-class education to children whose parents could never have afforded a private school. I was accepted to Wanstead County High School, farther away than my first school — a thirty-five-minute walk, or a bus or train or, more often than not, a quick cycle ride. It seemed big, slightly frightening, and far more adult than I'd been used to.

It was also where I was first told the basics of sex and procreation, but certainly not by a teacher. I was eleven, and a group of boys — it was co-ed, but there was very little mixing between the genders at this stage — were sitting around and discussing with a contrived and utterly false sense of confidence how the world worked, or didn't. Suddenly, Lawrence Hiller — still a good friend and someone who always seemed a little more knowing than the rest of us — asked rhetorically, "Do you lot know which part of a woman babies come from?"

I said confidently, "Ah, it's the bum, isn't it?"

The other boys nodded in agreement.

"No," he said, with the attitude of one who understood and had sympathy for my naïveté and was willing to gently correct me. "I used to think that, but it's not," and then he outlined how and where babies did actually enter the world.

I'm not sure how old he had been when he "used to think that," but I'm not sure either that I entirely believed him. Whenever I see

Lawrence in Britain, he continues to stand by his explanation of life's origins.

The mechanics of procreation aside, girls occupied an increasing area of my thoughts, imagination, and dreams. I had all sorts of largely innocuous and sometimes even charming fantasies about girls I was at school with, but it would be three years before I had the courage to actually ask one of them out on a date. Then there were the women teachers. When I look back, I suppose a lot of them were in their early twenties, attractive and interesting young women who had to teach classes in which half the students were boys with early puberty roaring through them and hormones dancing up a sensual storm. They knew, of course they knew, and it probably amused them more than anything else.

It's radically different now, with the ease of the internet and a far more open and permissive society, but in the early 1970s, the very idea of sex and physical contact with women seemed impossibly distant for us. I didn't kiss a girl until I was fourteen. Her name was Nicola, she had a twin, and we met in nearby Clayhall Park. It was a kiss and a grope, all very clumsy and as intimidating as it was pleasurable. We exchanged phone numbers and then went our separate ways. The next night she phoned my home and my mother answered while our family was having dinner. Mum came to the kitchen table with a huge smile on her face. "There's a young lady on the phone for you," she said. I remember blushing, as though a guilty secret had been discovered or I'd done something terribly wrong. Nicola and I arranged to meet again the next day in the same place, but I stood her up because there was a Jerry Lewis movie on the television, and it was years before we had access to videos and recording. Kissing and groping were, it seems, less of an attraction than a dated U.S. comic. The truth is, I think I was frightened.

There were some other very brief encounters, but for the most part my romantic life remained something of an empty vessel, even though we all thought and spoke about the subject. We boasted, too, but all knew that everyone was either lying or playing elaborate games with the truth. We were teenagers in the early 1970s and the most sexual images we ever saw were young women dancing on television, underwear ads in Sunday newspapers or in shopping magazines that would come into the house, or in the very occasional pornographic magazine that we found in dump sites on empty subway platforms. This last had always intrigued me. Who left them there, and why? Of the two or three I ever saw, one of them was a publication called *Health and Efficiency* or, as we called it, *H&E*. It was actually a nudist magazine — they prefer the word "naturist" — and was apparently devoted to travel, health, and general well-being for people who liked to be naked. The pictures of women without any clothes on were often far from the fantasies we imagined, and for some reason they were usually playing with beachballs or holding tennis rackets. Still, desperate times and all that.

We did have more than our fair share of scandals at Wanstead. In 1973, three years after I'd started at the school, our highly regarded headteacher, Donald Mackay, became the subject of intense media coverage. He had had a relationship with a young woman in the sixth form, so I assume she was seventeen or eighteen. He was a much older man, but charismatic and attractive in a certain way. It was consensual but obviously inappropriate. Journalists from the popular press crowded at the school gates asking us whether we knew anything about what was going on. We didn't but wished that we did, and before social media and twenty-four-hour news, it remained a mystery for most of us. That didn't, naturally, prevent us from becoming overnight experts.

Far more sinister, and certainly criminal, was the case of music teacher Michael Crombie, whose behaviour was gossiped about when I was at the school but didn't become public knowledge until after I'd left. He was eventually sent to prison for three years after admitting to forty-seven counts of indecently assaulting children between 1964 and 1993. The judge who sentenced him said there had been numerous complaints over the years. All I remember is one of the girls in my class saying, "You know that Mr. Crombie? He's a right bleeding wanker, if you ask me."

□

Passing the eleven-plus and going to a grammar school meant a new class experience for most of us, and certainly for me. Most of my contemporaries were from a similar background, but we were assumed to be clever and thus somehow different from the places and people we'd come from. Different meant better. This wasn't a private school but acted as one. We were all in different houses, named after royal dynasties; uniforms were strictly enforced; and we even played different sports. Boys played soccer, were obsessed with it, had teams they were committed to, and even dreamed of one day playing for professionally — none of us ever did. That was about to change. During our first gym class at Wanstead, a Welsh sports teacher came in. He was very loud and strict and slightly terrifying and made it abundantly clear that from now on we would play rugby, and soccer was all but banned. Rugby was a passion in Wales, and a different version of the game in the northwest of England, but back then — and even today, to a lesser extent — it was the sport of private schools and the middle and upper class. That was what we now had to aspire to: a different game for a different social group. It was an outward feature of the inner divisions that plagued British society. We did what we were told, grew to like the game, and were sometimes even quite good at it — we produced one England player. I was big enough and nasty enough to make the first team. But it was an artificial creation, and we all reverted to soccer as soon as we went to the local park.

We were also encouraged to play cricket, but to a lesser extent because it's a summer game and we, of course, were on holiday during the summer. Nevertheless, I developed a passion for the game and would watch my local team, Essex, whenever I could. When the Australian national team toured England in 1972, I went to nearby Valentines Park with some friends to watch them play Essex. At the lunch interval, I waited close to where the players were leaving the field, and when one of Australia's stars came close to me, I politely asked him for his autograph. He replied, "Fuck off, lad." The words were hardly new to me, but I was still shocked that a world-famous international athlete would use them to dismiss a thirteen-year-old boy. He could have said "no" or simply ignored me.

When I got home, my dad asked me about the game. I told him about it, and also explained what had happened. He was much angrier than I was, and after the weekend tracked down where the Australian team was staying, managed somehow to contact one of the team's staff, and demanded an apology. The man, though not the culprit, did indeed apologize, said that it had happened too many times, and sent me the autographs of the entire team. I lost the thing over the years and wish that I hadn't. The man who swore at me is now seventy-seven years old. I wonder if he still tells polite thirteen-year-olds to fuck off.

The education at Wanstead was generally very good, and I even grew to respect and like my gym teacher. Two teachers, however — a Mr. Doyle for English and a Mr. Smethurst for history — changed my life. I wish I'd been able to tell them that directly. Doyle, who for some obscure reason we called "Bugsy" (never in his hearing), showed me the beauty of the English language and introduced me to its finest exponents. It was in his classes that I began to love Shakespeare, Wordsworth, Keats,

Dickens, Orwell, and so many others. In history classes, where most of my friends were bored, I was for some reason captivated by the past and how it shaped everything around us. In particular, our year spent on sixteenth-century England left in me a life-long obsession. It also built another step in my journey toward Christianity. We spent months reading and learning about the Reformation, a subject I'd never encountered before I was twelve years old. Why would I have? That there were such differences in belief surrounding Christianity, that they were so interesting, that people even thought about these things at all stimulated something in me that has never disappeared.

There were the other teachers, though. I didn't get into fights very often, but one day a rather odd classmate made some sort of comment that offended me, because that was what he had intended it to do. We wrestled and punched as a crowd formed around us. He then tried to stab me with a pair of compasses, which I thought was a bit much, but then nobody ever said that geometry was safe. A young teacher ran into the circle, dragged us apart — which, if we'd been honest, we both wanted — and then frogmarched us up to see the housemaster. He ran into the room and punched us both in the back of the head. Hard. There was no lasting damage, physically or otherwise, but what I've always remembered is that none of us present — me, the other boy, the teacher — thought this in any way unusual.

There were also the young, idealistic teachers who meant so well but tried to be friends rather than authority figures. No punches from them, but not much discipline, either. There was a middle way between angry violence and callow attempts at egalitarianism. I'm ashamed to say that we often made their lives absolutely awful.

□

It was 1973 and I was fourteen years old when I had my first en-counter with death. Teenagers consider themselves immortal, which meant that when a schoolfriend was hit by a car and killed, I had no idea how to react and what to feel. The funeral seemed so foreign to me, like a sickening interruption in my emotional diary. Sorrow, fear, or just profound confusion? As I was leaving the cemetery, looking at the ground and trying not to cry, I found myself walking alongside the local Church of England priest who'd taken the cere-mony. He came in to the school sometimes to teach some classes, but we didn't know him at all well. He saw my obvious discomfort and asked if I was okay. I replied with a teenaged mumble. "Don't worry," he said, "I won't try to convert you. I'm here to chat if you need to. But please never think that you're on your own in this. If my faith tells me anything, it's that. We're all in this together."

It wasn't profound — perhaps it was even banal, in a caring way — and I certainly didn't consciously reflect on what he said. Yet I don't think I ever quite forgot it, either. I later found out that the young cleric was a noted classicist and scholar. He could, therefore, have given me all sorts of theology and philosophy, little of which I would have understood. He said what he did because it had a pristine and fierce wisdom and because it was the right thing to say.

Almost fifty years later, I attended a school reunion in a Wanstead pub and saw lots of old — and, sadly, I mean *old*— faces. I also saw the girls with whom I was in love at school and who are now grandmas themselves. Over in a corner was a man likely in his mid- or even late seventies, wearing a clerical collar. I looked harder and thought I recognized him. He was different, but not dramat-ically so. Then I realized it was the priest from the funeral. He'd apparently helped some of the friends of the boy who had died and had stayed in contact with the school for years afterward. That day, he'd been invited along as part of the community.

I approached him. "You probably don't remember me," I said.

He smiled. "Yes, I do. You're Michael. I met you back in 1973 at the funeral. I told you that we're not alone in this, and I've prayed for you ever since then."

A pause, as I stood there amazed and speechless.

Then he said, "I heard you'd become a writer — I've read some of your work, actually. But I also heard that you had been ordained in the church in Canada."

I said that I was, that I am.

"That's good," he said. "That's really very good. You see, I told you that we're never alone."

I wish I'd known and felt that, back then. I wish I'd known and felt that so many times in my life.

□

School offered myriad opportunities, few of which I took advantage of. That's been a running theme in my life and is a purely self-inflicted wound. I began to develop a laziness that has plagued me. People sometimes think I'm prolific and hard-working, but that's largely an illusion. At school, when I was fourteen, I regarded myself as a rebel and as being tough. I was neither. My parents had grown up in genuinely rough circumstances, in parts of London that had produced notorious gangs and gangsters. Not me. Violence was uncommon at school, but we played at it. When there were fights, they were usually brief, and nobody was seriously hurt. Not always, though. There was little anti-Semitism at Wanstead, other than one or two boys who made the occasional snide comment, but one day, one of the larger boys was called a "bloody Jew" by a particularly unpleasant teenager. The bloody Jew in question turned around and landed a punch on the abuser's chin so hard that the little racist fell unconscious. None of us had ever seen that before, outside of boxing on television or in cartoons. Everybody seemed to be silent for a few moments, and then the boy who had made the comment came to, shook his head, and wandered off. There were no repercussions, no detentions, no investigations.

I went through phases, as all teenagers do. And they are just that: phases. My dad was a supporter of Tottenham soccer club, and so was I. A bit about Tottenham, because this still matters to me. Tottenham Hotspur, also known as Spurs, is a big, wealthy, north London club. It was dominant at one time and has won many trophies, and while the former glory days haven't quite returned, it's always been an important player in world soccer. It's also regarded by some as "the Jewish team," and if you listen carefully to their games on television, you'll hear their fans chanting, "Yids, Yids" or "Yid Army, Yid Army." This was less the case back in the early and mid-1970s, but it's been an issue for many years. Tottenham always had a large number of Jewish supporters, because the catchment area for the club has a sizable Jewish community. Yet until relatively recently, there were no Jewish owners of the team, and over the years, there has been only one Jewish manager (or coach) and perhaps four or five Jewish players.

The point of transition is layered in irony and centres on a television show called *Till Death Us Do Part*, the inspiration for the American comedy *All in the Family*. The anti-hero was the character Alf Garnett, a racist and a bigot who followed east London's West Ham United team and disliked almost everyone, including Tottenham and "the Jews up at Spurs." Garnett was the symbol of all that was wrong, stupid, and undesirable, but nevertheless, his opinions had a certain appeal to some. The irony I spoke of is that Alf Garnett was played by the Jewish actor and life-long Tottenham fan Warren Mitchell. At Wanstead, most boys were West Ham fans.

In the 1970s, the far right in Britain made a concerted attempt to recruit among soccer hooligans. Groups such as the National

Front and British Movement, always small and never a genuine political threat, still caused trouble and were vocal and visible. At Chelsea and West Ham, they had some success. At Chelsea in particular, there was an organized fascist minority, and when they shouted, "Yids, Yids," they meant it. Worse, they also sang, "We've never felt more like gassing the Jews," and even, during a Spurs game against Chelsea, made hissing sounds that were supposed to indicate the noise of Nazi gas chambers. Such obscenities have been illegal for some years, so now it's rare — though far from unknown — for anybody else in a stadium other than Tottenham supporters to chant "Yids." Spurs fans have owned the word, taken possession of it, and refuse to give it up.

This was the context of me as a Spurs fan in the early 1970s. I'd go to home games, and some away ones, in my DMs (Doc Marten boots), Sherman shirts, and either a Harrington jacket or a Crombie coat. A Tottenham scarf would be wrapped around my neck, and I'd be with my friends at the back of crowds of young men chanting and shouting. I was actually terrified that the fighting would reach me, but it never really did. I played the part, acted the role of a hooligan. The only time I was ever hurt was during a game against our hated rival, Arsenal, when a policeman pulled me up by the neck, effectively hanging me for a few moments, with the words, "Come here, ginger," and then threw me back into the crowd.

I should explain that until I was in my early twenties, I had red hair — had hair at all! Curly, ginger hair, the same colour as my dad, and his mum before him.

The soccer thug disappeared as quickly as it had arrived, and then came the knowing, cynical, clever, and incredibly annoying fifteen- and sixteen-year-old. The uniform changed to army surplus greatcoats, looks of cultivated indifference, and carrying albums under my arms by bands that were considered more sophisticated than the Top Twenty music most of the class was listening to. Emerson, Lake & Palmer; Focus; or even, at a pinch, Deep Purple: "Yeah, but they've sold out." I never knew precisely what "selling out" was, but it was likely connected to commercial success.

I took up playing the drums and was rather good at it. I'd listen to long drum solos and try to emulate them on my kit in the attic in my parents' house. I now realize how patient they were with so much noise coming from the top of their home. The drums were good but too big to transport.

The alto saxophone came next, and I worked all through summer holidays and weekends to buy a Selmer Mark VI, which was regarded as the prince of the instrument. The saxophone required actual lessons and the ability to read music. That lasted for a year or so, but I never came to like jazz and never have, so I was limited in what I could play. I sold the sax and bought a bass guitar, because I thought it would be easier to learn than a lead guitar and was crucial to a rock band. I became bored of that, too. My music career, though not my love of music, came to an end. These days, the only time I perform live on stage in front of thousands is when I'm alone in the car on the highway with AC/DC turned up loud on the radio.

As I abandoned music, I became interested in politics. I'm not sure why, because my family and friends weren't especially political. The process and the mechanics fascinated me, and I saw my love of history in living forms within the political machines and personalities. Soccer and music seemed so meagre compared with government, and I wondered if the political life would suit me. As soon as I met politicians and saw the reality of how it all worked, that interest would end, and I've always been glad it did. But my teachers were encouraging me to go to university, and rather than study history — which I should have — I decided to find a politics course.

My parents, as always, encouraged me, too. Encouragement was what they did. They thought it was a good idea to study politics, even though they had no idea what a politics degree was all about.

A note on my parents before I move on. They would both live into their early seventies, and I wish I could have told them more of how I felt. Then again, I could have told them if I'd really wanted to do so. The opportunity was there and there's nobody to blame but myself. Even now, there's something in me that goes beyond the natural grab and grip of pain but is something sharper and darker. A spinning combination of guilt, self-realization, and sobering nostalgia.

Guilt because I took my mother and my father for granted. Yes, yes, that's supposed to be the way, but my children treat their parents with far greater awareness than I did mine. I loved them, I told them I loved them, but did I show them that I loved them? When I blithely left for Canada to marry a woman I'd met in Toronto, I didn't give my parents a second thought. Of course, they wanted me to be happy, encouraged me, but everything I did was defined by my needs and my wants.

And self-realization because as I grow older, as a father and now grandfather, I've come to understand what family and sacrifice are about, and to relish the star-soaked symbiosis of relationships. I failed at that. No, I'm not being too hard on myself — I'm being honest. The self-realization that floods me isn't comfortable, and it opens wounds that were never healed but only ignored and forgotten. The pain is suddenly reignited, and the tears I have are as much self-pity as sorrow for Mum and Dad. So, once again, it's about me. Damn it, it's again about me.

This is all tied in with a sense of mortality. There was once a time when I never discussed health with friends. Now it's often the first subject we speak about. Death doesn't frighten me — my faith is strong, I think — but not being able to see my children and their children grow to maturity certainly does. As it must have frightened my parents, whose concerns I failed to grasp and didn't even try to because of my lack of empathy. If I were writing from an experience of familial abuse or neglect, it would be more linear — horrible but clearer. No. My parents cared for me, protected me, and gave what they could seldom afford to make my life easier. God in Heaven, I should have acknowledged that so much more energetically and enthusiastically.

They gave me crimsons, purples, and royal blues, and I replied with the greys and browns of complacency. Now they rest in dull, colourless places and I want so much to put it all right, and to repair the damage. It can't be done, at least not in this thin land of waiting. I sincerely believe in an eternal life, and perhaps other words and other gestures can be made in times to come. I should have done and been better, could have done and been better, and now look for forgiveness rather than sympathy. As a Christian priest, I'm in the forgiving business, but this is something beyond my control.

I'm sorry, Mum. I'm sorry, Dad.

I loved and love you.

# CHAPTER TWO

---

# UNIVERSITY CHALLENGED

I left Wanstead High School in 1977 and lost contact with most of my contemporaries. One couple has always stood out for me, however, as they did for most people back then. I say "couple," because Jonathan and Angela seemed to have always been partners, even when we were sixteen. I remember them because they were remarkable, in almost every sense. Angela was beautiful, clever, and a gifted athlete. Jonathan was annoyingly handsome, also clever, and a superb rugby player. In other words, they seemed to have everything. And to make matters worse, they were also very nice. It should go without saying that if people have so many qualities, they should at least be arrogant and unpleasant so that others can feel justified in resenting them. But these two weren't.

We all parted ways and went off to work or university, and I didn't think about them until a mutual friend told me about a reunion party at their apartment. Apparently, they'd been living abroad and had recently returned. I received the invitation.

Attached to it was a note, explaining some things. They'd lived in central Africa, where Angela had been a teacher at a small village school. One day the building had caught fire, and Jonathan had rushed in to save a little boy who was still trapped inside when everybody else had been evacuated. The boy, Joshua, was fine, but Jonathan had received some burns. They wanted people to know so we weren't shocked when we saw him.

It was 7 p.m. on a midsummer evening in west London. I pressed the buzzer and Angela, as beautiful as ever, opened the door. She said that I was the first to arrive and brought me in to meet Jonathan. There he sat, and he was beyond recognition. There was so much scar tissue on his face that I couldn't make out his features. I tried not to react, but obviously I did. Then the words came from him, and the voice hadn't changed one bit. "All right, Coren, I know I look a bloody mess," he said. "But at least one of us has kept his hair."

I tried to laugh, but instead choked up. Angela rushed to me, hugged me, and said it was okay, they'd both cried a lot, it was okay. Then a small African boy who had been shyly hiding in the kitchen suddenly jumped into Jonathan's lap and tickled him.

"This," said Angela, "is our new adopted son. His name is Joshua."

I then learned the whole story. These gorgeous, brilliant, good people were devout Christians — I hadn't known it back at school, because I simply hadn't listened or cared. They had gone to Africa not to convert anybody but for Jonathan to work as an engineer in the village, and Angela to teach. "You know," Angela said, "women used to walk past us and turn their heads to look at my husband. He was so good-looking. People still turn their heads to look now, but for a different reason. For me, though, he's more lovable and perfect than ever."

It's a story that shook me then and still does now, but this was still the me who was far more interested in what the world could offer than in people who believed in God and goodness. I admired their dedication, envied their love, but part of me reflected on the sacrifice they'd made and wondered if it had all been worthwhile. My tears were genuine, I cared and was touched, but emotion is never enough. We're creatures, we're influenced too easily by mood and immediacy, and something deeper is required for authentic change to take place.

□

Apart from anything else, there was university and all that it offered. Nobody in my family had ever attended university. My mother's family were poor and rural until the beginning of the twentieth century, and then they were poor and urban. Dad's clan were Jewish peasants in eastern Europe, so that made university equally impossible. Oxford or Cambridge was never going to happen for someone from my background, and we were never given the opportunity to apply.

At my school, even going to university was seen as unusual. Wanstead had changed from a grammar to a comprehensive school, which meant we were amalgamated with a local secondary school. The intentions were noble, and there's a strong argument to be made that separating children at the age of eleven based purely on intellectual status is a bad idea. But at Wanstead, we were an early attempt at the comprehensive model and were consequently caught in the middle of a social experiment. There were times of disorganization and confusion, and it definitely had an effect on our education. One boy in our year went to Cambridge, but he had long stood out as exceptional. Most of us applied to good alternatives, at a time when there were far fewer universities and a lot more polytechnics. I was accepted at all of the universities to which I applied — Warwick, Hull, Liverpool, and Lancaster — but decided on the University of

Nottingham because it had a very good reputation and its politics department was highly regarded. Over the years, I've developed a close relationship with Oxford, far closer than my relationship with Nottingham, but while I'm sure I could have coped with the intellectual demands of the place, which were not very different from any other leading university at the time, I would have been socially out of place and out of my depth.

The problem was that I'd read too much Evelyn Waugh and John Betjeman and expected dreaming spires and bright young things, but this wasn't Oxford or Cambridge. Mind you, I'm not sure that Oxford and Cambridge were actually Oxford and Cambridge by then. Nottingham had some beautiful buildings and was built on one of the loveliest campuses, a former park, in the country. I was given rooms in Sherwood Hall, named after one of the local areas but inevitably bringing the medieval outlaw to mind, although not as much as the city's Maid Marian Way and Robin Hood's Close.

The first person I met at the university was the student I was to share a room with for a year. We had our own bedrooms but a large, joint study that connected the two rooms. Our new home was larger than those in the rest of Sherwood Hall but that, we soon discovered, was because we were located on top of the central boiler. So, it was hot, too hot, all of the year, and even in winter we had our windows wide open.

When my new friend introduced himself, I assumed he was German or Dutch. It turned out he was from Blackburn in Lancashire. I'd hardly been to the north of England, other than for football matches or a holiday in the Lake District, and was genuinely bewildered by his accent.

The second thing he said turned out, after mild translation, to be, "Are ye a Christian?" Was I a Christian? No. And if anything was going to turn me away from any evangelistic efforts, it was a well-meaning but clumsy trainee social worker asking if I'd let Christ into my life.

In my first tutorial we discussed what we'd be studying in the following three years, and the seven or eight students explained to the professor, an enlightened and progressive Cambridge man, why they'd chosen to read for a politics degree. The first subject the tutor wanted to talk to us about was pre-war British fascism and its leader, the repugnant if gifted Sir Oswald Mosley, whose black-shirted followers would randomly attack Jewish people in London's East End. It was pure coincidence that this was a theme with personal connections, but I assumed everybody in the room had at least a passing knowledge of what had happened and would give some strong opinion or condemnation. There was a shocking lack of response — shocking to me and, I think, to the tutor as well. Perhaps it was shyness, but perhaps not.

Then one of the young men sitting around the table said, "We had that chap Mosley speak at our school once." He had been to one of Britain's more famous and expensive public schools. (I should explain that in a wonderfully obscure and confusing way, "public" schools are in fact private and very expensive. The term originates from the eighteenth century, when these institutions began to take in students from outside of the local area, who would board at the school.) There was silence. He'd made the comment so nonchalantly, as though it were entirely natural and objective to have an admirer of Hitler and Mussolini, a man who was imprisoned during the Second World War for reasons of national security, speak at his school as if he were a famous old boy or a local celebrity.

I broke the uncomfortable silence by asking if there were any Jewish children at the school.

Pause.

"I rather think there were," he drawled.

"How," I asked, "do you think they felt?"

His reply: "I have absolutely no idea."

No, he certainly didn't.

I joined various societies and also signed up for the Officers' Training Corps (OTC). This was similar to a militia, and required every Wednesday afternoon, some weekends, and a few days during the vacation for military training. There was a small stipend, we were given uniforms that seemed designed purposely to be uncomfortable, and were trained in the very basics of soldiering. I'm not very military, and while it was fun to run around and jump out of things, I knew that the army would never be a fit. It was for some of my friends in the OTC, however, and if they completed the course, they received some time off from training if they went to Sandhurst, the military college, to be made into real officers. Some of us were sent to an army parachute training school. "You'll enjoy it," I was told. I didn't. Some of those in the group relished every moment, but I was more frightened than I'd ever been. The training was very good, far better than most people receive, and it was a static line jump where no cords are pulled — unless the main canopy doesn't open and the reserve has to be used, which is very unusual and a terrifying idea. There's a sense of euphoria when you land, and if you do what you're told and roll properly with chin down, elbows in, feet and knees together, it's all relatively smooth. Then we had to do it again and again. It never became more enjoyable for me, and I was happy when it was all over.

After we'd completed the course and performed the required number of jumps, we all went out to celebrate, which meant getting absurdly drunk. I woke up the next morning with a tattoo of parachute wings on my lower arm, for which I'd never nor never would have given consent. It's low because the tattoo "artist" could roll my sleeve up only that far. They're not supposed to do these things to people who are semi-conscious, but my friends thought it would be great fun. I didn't share that opinion and nor did the two others who had also been tattooed. I eventually went to a dermatologist to see if it could be removed, and he was brutally honest: it would take several painful procedures, after which I'd have to keep it out of any sunlight, and even at the end of it all there would still be a clear outline. His advice was to leave it be.

It could have been worse. During the Second World War, my grandpa had my grandma's name, Bertha, tattooed on his arm. By the time I knew him it had faded, his skin had loosened, and it looked like "Bethin."

It was in the OTC that I had my only gay encounter. By "gay encounter," I mean that in a two-person tent one night, my fellow would-be officer put his arm over mine and asked if I'd be interested in what he described as "that." At first, I wasn't entirely sure what "that" was, but soon caught on. The whole thing was so very British. I said I was deeply flattered, didn't want to be rude in any way, but I was interested only in girls. I actually apologized to him. He was similarly courteous, and I still remember his words: "Fully understand — sorry to have asked. Have a good sleep." I'm not sure I did. That pleasant young man in the great tent exchange went on to become a surgeon who, I'm told, is renowned for his gentleness with patients and warmth toward their families.

My brief experience with the military, and homosexuality, left me with a respect and admiration for the soldiers I met. Occasionally we would perform operational exercises with the Territorial Army (TA), or Reserves, and the regular army. Regulars would sometimes refer contemptuously to the TA as Stabs — Stupid Territorial Army Bastards — which was deeply unfair. I came across a few people in the army, all men, who I thought were virtually psychotic and far too interested in violence as an end in itself, but for the most part, those in uniform were balanced and moderate people who found themselves in the services out of family tradition, a desire for adventure, lack of alternative job opportunities, or sheer circumstance.

Many had a genuine social conscience and a pronounced sense of justice and the need for right to triumph over wrong. We were given talks about the dangers of fascist extremism in the ranks, but I never saw anything even close to it. I appreciated the raw honesty and earthiness of the people I met, which was often so different from my fellow students at university.

There was quite a lot of that naïveté and unworldliness around back then at universities, and I was often taken aback at how little my fellow students knew about life beyond their own direct experience. The same undoubtedly applied to me, and there's always a temptation to assume that what we have known, seen, and felt is somehow superior and more important than what others have. It was in fact a time of incredible privilege for me. I received a full grant, meaning that all my tuition and rent were paid for. I even had some spending money on top of that, and my parents gave me what they could so I could live what was an incredibly easy life. I would come to see my children have to work so hard to help pay their university fees, and I meet students all the time who are taking on enormous debts as well as working two or more jobs. Not me, not then. I didn't appreciate how fortunate I was, but then solipsism is a favourite creature of youth.

Nor were my studies especially arduous. We began our three-year honours bachelor of arts degree with eight subjects, including U.S. legal history, Eurocommunism, the decline of the Spanish Empire, British local government (not a bag of laughs), and ancient political philosophy and theory. It was an eclectic and mostly interesting package. Each year we narrowed down the focus, until by the time I sat my finals in 1980, I was studying pure politics, with my thesis written on Lehi, better known — if they're remembered at all now — as the Stern Gang, an extremist Jewish underground movement active in 1940s Palestine. Having broken away from the Irgun, which had broken away from the mainstream Jewish and

Zionist community and organizations in pre-state Palestine, they were responsible for some appalling acts of terrorism and violence. It was a serious piece of work, during a three-year period when I didn't do that much serious work.

Part of my research involved spending almost a year in Israel, in 1979. It was my first visit, although I've been many times since. Because I'd grown up half-Jewish and outside of mainstream Jewish culture, I wasn't involved in visits to Israel, had no particular interest in the country, and felt little connection to it. My time there was transformative for me, and I think hope has always given me a balanced view of the reality of the situation. My first week there, I met a young woman from Cana in Galilee, with whom, I thought at the time, I'd spend the rest of my life. Layla was beautiful, intelligent, and one of the gentlest people I'd ever and have ever met. She was an Israeli Arab Christian, a Palestinian who had been included by various circumstances inside Israel in 1948. She'd been raised with Arabic and Hebrew, and her English was fluent. She lives in South America now and speaks perfect Spanish as well. She'd grown up with Jewish as well as Christian and Muslim friends, especially as a member of the educated middle class — her parents were both doctors. I'll always remember her saying to me about her place in Israeli society, "They lead us to water but they won't let us drink." She regarded herself as Israeli, had no desire to belong to another country, but wanted desperately for the country to change. Her heart must break now, because there was so much more hope for peace and equality forty-five years ago.

I asked her once what it was like growing up in Cana, which might be the place where Jesus performed his first miracle and turned water into wine. (I say "might be" because there are other claimants in the region to be the original Cana.) "When I was little I could never understand why all of these foreigners kept coming to our little town," she said. "All I wanted was to get out of it." We became a couple, we seemed inseparable, and Layla was even teaching me Arabic when she wasn't mocking my Hebrew. When I left Israel, we swore we'd maintain our relationship and she'd come to Britain to visit. We wrote a few letters, but phone calls were expensive and difficult, there was no Zoom or Facebook, and we gradually drifted apart. My heart broke a little, but then hearts at that age are supposed to do so. There were echoes of a later long-distance relationship, but one that would have different results.

My time there, and my time with Layla, has always made me suspicious of instant experts on the Middle East, and certainly of people who seem to have extreme motives. The inescapable truth is that if European Christians had acted in the genuine spirit of Jesus, there would have been no expulsions of Jews, no mass slaughters, no blood libels, no pogroms, and no Holocaust. Anti-Semitism was an open wound in Europe for almost two thousand years, and still screams its horrors. If Jewish people had been treated properly, it is unlikely Israel would have come into being in 1948. The Jews cried out for a homeland where they could have dignity and safety, but the resulting birth defect of that event was the expulsion and oppression of the Palestinian people. Jews are indigenous to Israel, but in the hiatus between their expulsion and their return, a new people had settled. They are Palestinians. There are two truths in existence in Israel and Palestine, and they have lived and died together for more than seventy-five years, with each new outrage being merely a symptom of the original injustice. There's a litany of realities that are often overlooked. The Palestinians have been and are treated terribly. The Arab states have been hypocritical and unethical, often suppressing their own people as badly — and sometimes worse. Some in the Muslim world boast fraternity with Palestine but govern Muslims in their own states as cruel despots.

Anti-Semitism is filthy, and even Jewish people indifferent to the Middle East have been its victims, especially when there is tension in the region. The United States, and the former Soviet Union, use the region for proxy war, testing out their weapons, more concerned with power and politics than humanity and morality. I honestly don't see any short-term solution to the quagmire, but I'm always astounded at the decency of most people on all sides. It won't be solved by hard-left platitudes or hard-right blindness, but by something far more complex and revolutionary. Taking absolute positions is easy and comfortable, but ultimately pointless. In the short term, we can work to criminalize the arms trade, oblige all governments to abide by international agreements and human rights codes, make religion irrelevant for citizenship qualification, invest enormously into regional infrastructure, and reward those who genuinely pursue peace rather than war. Whether any of that will happen, I don't know, and in my darker moments, I very much doubt.

I returned from Israel for my final year at university feeling very grown up and worldly. I wasn't. I also encountered drugs for the first time. I'm sure there were hard drugs around, but until that time, I had been exposed only to cannabis and magic mushrooms. I'd never smoked cigarettes, so pot was difficult to take, and the idea of cannabis candy was a long way off in an English provincial town. Magic mushroom tea was okay, but only a select few of us knew which mushrooms to pick, and the results were unpredictable. I remember one friend spending the night sitting on the bed, terrified that something was about to come out of the wall and attack him. So, the effects were inconsistent and sometimes unpleasant, and it was too much of an effort just for a few hours of fantasy.

What I did take, and now regret, were methamphetamines, or speed. In my second and third year I lived off campus, and there was a local who supplied the students. I tried speed because a friend used it and told me how much energy he had and how confident and happy it had made him feel. The first time I took it was before what we called a "Week One Disco," which now sounds as archaic as something out of a Victorian novel. These events took place in large halls where new and existing students would dance under flashing lights to bad disco music. It was a chance to meet young women, but I was always nervous. Alcohol helped, but the first time I was given speed, I suddenly had the confidence of an army. The little pill flushed me with energy and enthusiasm. And boy, how I could dance! (Very badly.) It worked in a way because I felt able to approach women and start conversations, and sometimes secure a few dates.

But that feeling became addictive, and I wanted and needed to make it happen again. The side effects were unpleasant but not impossible: an inability to sleep until the middle of the night, a constant need to drink water and so to pee, the desire to make pointless lists and put things in order — whatever that meant to a nineteen-year-old with hardly any genuine responsibilities. I'm convinced that it had a lasting effect on my brain chemistry. Not that I have any of those feelings now, but for the first few months after quitting, I had headaches and mild depression. Coming off wasn't easy, even though I'd been told by alleged friends that the drug could be kicked at any time. There are more addictive substances, but I made a conscious decision to stop after I woke up in a public washroom lying in my own or someone else's urine. I'd drunk too much alcohol after popping a pill and that was the result.

I could usually get away with bad or stupid behaviour because I was clever. Not outstanding but well read, quick, and sharp. That became obvious when the university entered something called *University Challenge*, a weekly television show where students from competing universities would appear to answer a whole circus of general-knowledge questions and progress accordingly, perhaps to the final. There was a university-wide competition to find the five best students (four to be on screen, with one reserve). I made the top five, though was the reserve for all of our games. That annoyed me because I know I did better than one of the other four, who had friends in the right places. Still, it meant trips to Granada Studios in Manchester, touring the set of *Coronation Street*, and being paid. Our fee increased each time we won, and we won several games before being beaten by Queen's University in Belfast. I managed to get into the team the following year as well, but this time we didn't do as well.

I became very close friends with another member of the team and would eventually be best man at his first wedding. That was John Hayes, who would go on to become a Conservative MP, a minister in various government departments, and a privy councillor, and to be knighted. He's also one of the most right-wing members of the House of Commons, and last time we met I was astounded at the lack of change in most of his views. We were genuinely close for many years; his eccentricity and humour could be compelling. He's a kind man — I've seen many examples of that — but his politics are bizarre and disturbing. I shared some of them once, but hope I've grown up and changed.

John and I were friends with one of our professors, a generous and deeply interesting man named David Regan, who was close to the Margaret Thatcher government and connected to various political bodies. When I graduated in the summer of 1980, David asked me to go for a walk with him. He put his arm through mine, and we strolled across the university's startlingly green and leafy campus.

"So," he began, "do you have any idea what you'd like to do in life?"

I mumbled that I hadn't.

"Well," the highly influential academic responded, "you're very lazy and very clever. I suggest either journalism or espionage."

Slightly embarrassed by the whole thing, I gave some vaguely grateful answer about perhaps becoming a journalist and thought nothing more about it.

In 2009, Sir Robert John Sawers, who is four years older than me but was at Nottingham University at a similar time, was named chief of the Secret Intelligence Service, better known as MI6. Eugene Curley, CMG, OBE, was in my year at Nottingham, and I knew him. He was also a senior intelligence officer and is listed by his company as having led "operations in over seventy countries, was inter alia Head of Counter Terrorism and Head of the Foreign Service's effort on crime, fraud and money laundering." Pure coincidence that both these men were in David Regan's sphere of influence, or an attempt at recruitment? I don't know and likely never will. I do know that I would have made a terrible spy.

The idea of journalism had already started to occur to me. Johnny Margolis, the brother-in-law of a university friend, was a reporter on the *Yorkshire Post* in Leeds. I found Johnny fascinating. He made journalism sound compelling and exciting: chasing a story, finding facts that others hadn't come across, and presenting the whole thing to a mass audience with clarity and style. His writing, his approach, and his sheer interest in so many different and various subjects — what he called, in the best sense, "a butterfly mind" — won me over. To prove that point, Johnny would go on to write biographies of people as diverse as John Cleese, Michael Palin, Billy Connolly, and Uri Geller. He remains a dear friend.

At the time I first got to know him, Johnny — like so many other journalists — was working on a subject that held a dark dominance over domestic news: the murderer who was known as the Yorkshire Ripper. Because Johnny worked on the *Yorkshire Post*, a highly respected regional daily and arguably the best non-London newspaper in England, he was privy to details of the case that not everybody knew. He would be a contributor to one of the books that were written about the appalling story. The killer was eventually exposed as Peter William Sutcliffe, who died in prison in 2020. He was convicted of murdering thirteen women and attempting to murder seven others between 1975 and 1980. One of his victims, in 1979, was a twenty-year-old student named Barbara Leach. Her body was found close to the university lodgings where she lived, under a pile of bricks. It was grotesque. It also became grimly personal, in that later in that same year, I started a relationship with a fellow student named Lauris, who had been close friends with Barbara. My partnership with Lauris lasted only a month but it was a deeply significant one for me in all sorts of ways. Through her I saw the effect of these ghastly crimes not just on family but on friends: the tears, the fears, the pain, and the imagining.

It had an effect on me, too, and while reflecting on death and dying isn't advisable for people aged nineteen and twenty — there's plenty of time for that later — I'd been exploring religion and faith for some time. It had begun so many years earlier with Miss Power reading C.S. Lewis to the class and was sparked when I studied the Reformation as a teenager and had never completely disappeared. I was like someone standing on the beach as the tide slowly comes in. My feet are dry, then the first few waves cover my shoes, then the water hits my shins, then my waist, and finally I'm floating. The full float would take a few more years, and I'd been put off the church by my first-year roommate. He was nice enough in his own way, but apart from that impenetrable accent, his evangelical faith led him to be what I can only describe as manipulative. On the third day I was at university, I was feeling predictably homesick, and he asked if I'd like to go to a movie being shown on campus that night. "It's not a Christian thing, is it?" I asked. He assured me that it wasn't. I went along. It was. Worse, it was about a student who'd arrived at university and whose parents were killed in a car accident while he was away. That, and the ever-present smiles, were too much for me.

Anglicanism had very little presence at the university — or at least I wasn't aware of it, which is surprising because until 2019,

St John's College, only about eight miles away, was a thriving and well-known centre for Anglican and interdenominational education in the evangelical tradition. Methodism was around somewhere, but Roman Catholicism was always making some noise or other. I went to see the local Catholic priest, who was refreshingly different from the evangelicals I'd met. He was deeply intelligent, smoked a pipe, drank single malt scotch, and liked to tell stories, all of them allegedly true. There was one about a man who went to confession and in the booth told the priest that he'd had an argument with someone who had said some vile and obscene things about the Virgin Mary.

"What should I have done?" asked the man.

"You should have called him a damned swine," replied the priest, almost shouting out the two words. "You're a damned swine!"

When the man left, he had to walk past a line of waiting people, who stared at him incredulously. What had this "damned swine" done to provoke such a response?

There was another, a joke that no evangelical would ever tell. He poured me a whisky, chatted about transubstantiation, and then began. "Sister Mary Immaculate wakes up in the convent and walks along the corridor. The first nun she sees says, 'Someone got out of bed the wrong side this morning.' Sister Mary ignores her, because she has no idea what she's talking about. Then another nun passes her, and she too says, 'Someone got out of bed on the wrong side this morning.' At this point, Sister Mary is annoyed but still has no idea why this is happening. Then a third nun walks past and says, 'Someone got out of bed ...' At which point Sister Mary stops her and shouts, 'What is your problem? I'm smiling, I'm happy, I'm clean and washed — why do people keep telling me I got out of bed on the wrong side!' There's a pause. Then the other nun replies, 'Because you've got the bishop's shoes on.'"

I liked him.

I attended mass a few times, read the books that were recommended, and tried to pray, and I still think there was something that stuck. But I was too isolated, had no friends who were Christian, and was surrounded by people who assumed religion to be a hiding place for the unthinking and the unsophisticated. I wasn't dissuaded by atheism but battered by indifference. I developed the idea that if it did matter, if it was true, it could wait for later. I was too young and too busy to deal with it all then. There's an exchange in C.S. Lewis's *The Screwtape Letters,* in which a senior and junior devil discuss how to best prevent people from becoming Christian. At one point a young man realizes that faith is very important. One of the devils manages to convince him to conclude, "Quite. In fact, much too important to tackle at the end of a morning," and then has him go out to look for a

A very proud mum on the day her son graduated with a B.A. I was hungover.

place to eat. "Once he was in the street, the battle was won," explains the devil. I've no idea if anyone or anything cared about my spiritual formation, but I know that I left Nottingham University with little if any connection to organized religion, or very much explicit interest in faith.

When I told the Catholic priest that I might not be attending mass for a while, he was gracious and understanding; he had likely had this experience many times before. I wasn't baptized, had not had any formal classes with him, so all of this was still rudimentary. He told me that his door was always open, and that faith was a road and not an arrival, and then told me another joke. I wish I could remember what it was.

Shortly before I graduated in 1980, I was offered a place at Cambridge as a postgraduate. I've often wondered whether I should have accepted, and I do have regrets. It would have put me on a path to becoming an academic, but I don't think I would have been very good at it. I've now given many lectures across North America and Britain, and I preach most weeks, but these are one-off events, and the idea of repeated classes year after year wouldn't have suited me. In any case, I'd fallen for journalism, and I was already trying my hand at writing articles and becoming familiar with the work of journalists I particularly admired.

Back then, only two universities offered graduate courses in journalism: Cardiff University in Wales, and City University in London. I applied to the latter and managed to get in. More than that, I was given a full scholarship and had all of my tuition paid. That was no easy achievement, as it was a small class, most people who applied were rejected, and not all of those who were accepted were given grants. It was an impressive bunch of young people. There was the daughter of a leading Irish politician, the daughter of the British ambassador to first Greece and then the Soviet Union — people with all sorts of impressive connections and qualifications, including one who would become a good friend, Robert Winder, who had a first-class degree from Oxford and was charming and deeply intelligent.

Shortly before I started the course at City, I began to be published. I'd submitted one or two short articles to various magazines, but no one had bitten. Then, in 1981, the prestigious *New Statesman* magazine accepted a short piece I'd written about racism in British soccer. It was a subject I knew a little about, and after interviewing several Black players about their experiences, I wrote an article on the old manual typewriter my parents had given me and managed to put together something that made a few solid arguments. This was pre-internet and pre–online articles, and the print edition was everything. I woke early on the day of publication, cycled at first light to the closest store that stocked the magazine, and bought three copies. I was twenty-one years old and had my first article published, and in a magazine that had included some of the greats of English literature and letters. I remember when the cheque arrived. Being paid to write — just like Shakespeare, really. Or at least, that was how it felt.

Shakespeare, however, never had his writing quoted by the chair of the Football League in the *Evening Standard*, a mass-circulation London newspaper. When I saw this had happened, I managed to track down the league chairman and ask for an interview. He agreed, and I wrote a follow-up column for the *Statesman* on how seriously the authorities were taking the problem. Actually, they didn't take it very seriously at all, took decades to do much about it, and even now are often far too placid in their response. Still, I was a published journalist and had a relationship with an important national magazine.

I was also writing a regular interview column for *National Student*, the newspaper of the National Union of Students. This was a large and well-resourced organization to which almost every student in the country was obliged to belong. The paper was distributed nationwide, and I suggested a regular page where I interviewed people of interest, including the boxing champion, football stars, television pundits, authors, politicians, and various public figures. I was also offered a full-time job working for a newspaper. It was not, however, the sort of job I was thinking of. My name had been suggested to a very small newspaper called the *Goole Times*, a weekly in the East Riding of Yorkshire. It was the oldest and longest-serving weekly newspaper in Yorkshire, but when I went for an interview, I found it seemed to be located above a candy store. They offered me the job of sports editor but covering not the bigger soccer clubs of Hull City (thirty miles away) or even Leeds United (thirty-six miles) but Goole Town, a semi-professional team that has never been promoted to the Football League, the top four divisions of the professional sport. The editor and his small staff were very kind and encouraging and I genuinely considered taking the job, but I couldn't see how I could ever move to Goole. I was being offered a full-time job in journalism at twenty-one years old, but it seemed a step backward, so I politely turned it down. I remember someone there being quite angry, and saying something like, "You'll never work in this town again." Oddly enough, he was absolutely right.

When I say that my name had been suggested, I should mention what the name "Coren" meant in the media world back then. Alan Coren was an enormously respected and admired journalist, author, and broadcaster. He was editor of *Punch* and then the *Listener*, a columnist for the *Times*, the *Observer*, the *Sunday Express*, and the *Tatler*, a critic for the *Mail on Sunday*, and the author of several best-selling books. He was a regular panellist on a number of BBC television shows, wrote scripts, and in 1973 became rector of the University of St. Andrews, succeeding John Cleese. He was immensely clever, funny, and wise. He was also my cousin. Not a close cousin, but my parents were at his bar mitzvah, there was always contact, and when I decided on a career in journalism, he was extremely helpful as a guide and friend.

It wasn't that Alan found me a job — I was still the son of Phil the cabbie — but the name is uncommon, and in the Britain of the 1980s I would almost always be asked if I was related to Alan. He died in 2007, far too young, at the age of sixty-nine. I'll always remember something he said to me when my first book was published. It wasn't, in all honesty, a very good book, but Alan came to the dinner where we launched it and saw that I wasn't as celebratory as I should have been. He asked me why. I told him that I'd just seen an early review in a national Sunday paper, and it was awful. Others were different, with the *Guardian* being particularly enthusiastic and praising, but we always remember the bad ones. Alan said, "Keep writing. Keep bloody writing. That's the way to respond. They want to hurt you, want to stop you, so by not giving up writing, you win. And you'll get over it, believe me — you'll get over it." He was right. He generally was.

This all meant that when I arrived at City University, I had a small but noticeable reputation. I've never been certain whether my classmates resented that, but I generally got on well with them. There was one young man from an extremely privileged background who told the only Jewish girl in the class a joke that he thought would be amusing. It concerned Jewish victims of the Nazi death camps and how, unlike pizzas, they screamed when put into ovens. It was another example of something I've encountered numerous times over the years, where people aren't anti-Semitic as such but have absolutely no understanding of how offensive they can be, or of the effect their comments have on others. This man was socially dense, almost a caricature of a privately educated twit, but he would have been shocked if accused of racism. He was certainly shocked when the young Jewish woman, me, and the two non-Jewish people who were present told him what an arse he was. He's gone on to become a successful journalist.

The classes weren't unhelpful, but this was the early 1980s, when journalism, like everything else, was changing with a frightening and confusing speed. We had a weekly class in shorthand, parts of which I still remember, and I've never ever used it in my more than forty years of journalism. There was also a class in the history of journalism — interesting but of little practical use — and another on journalism and the law that would be of some help. By far the best part of it all were the classes in journalistic writing, where we used as biblical guidance a book called *Newsman's English*, by the revered editor of the *Sunday Times*, Harold Evans.

The guest lectures varied but could be immensely valuable in that we were hearing first-hand accounts of what it was like to cover every sort of story, to listen to people who had been there and done it. In an earlier year, the award-winning foreign correspondent John Pilger had come in to speak to us. He was well known in Britain as a bitingly tough left-wing critic of U.S., U.K., and Western foreign policy. He'd reported extensively from international conflicts, particularly in Vietnam; presented dozens of television documentaries; and, with his copious blond hair, great height, and Australian accent, was one of the most recognizable journalists in the country. He won Britain's Journalist of the Year award in 1967 and 1979 and is the author of many books. One of them would be co-written with me.

One morning, I was in the *Daily Mirror* building, trying to sell a story to an editor at the paper. In the elevator was John Pilger. This is where certain skills that can't be taught in journalism school come into play. I was confident and ambitious. In other words, I was pushy. I introduced myself, told John what I did, and said I was a great admirer of his work. Unlike my last contact with a famous Australian back on the cricket pitch in Ilford, he didn't tell me to go forth and multiply, but was polite and encouraging. "Send me some of your writing — love to see it," he said. I did, and within a week he called me at my parents' home, where I'd gone back to live and would do so until I bought my own tiny apartment in central London. Most days I'd cycle the eleven miles from their home in Ilford to central London, and eleven miles back again, because it saved money. John said on the phone that he'd read the handful of articles I'd now written for the *New Statesman*, and some others for a short-lived publication called the *East End News*, where I'd written on the far right in the area and some of the politics involving immigration and race. He said he'd liked them very much and asked to meet me. He was also, I later found out, taken with my being different from so many other young journalists who'd approached him. I was more working class, he said, more direct. I'm not sure if all that was true — or fair to others — but it worked for me.

We met, and he asked me to work as his researcher on some future projects and on a television show he was planning. Well, of course I would. This wasn't Goole — this was something entirely different. Terrifying but different.

I met with some friends at a pub to celebrate. As I was walking home, I realized I'd left my bag behind. I rushed back, but it was gone. There wasn't too much in it and I still had my wallet, but there were some personal items, notebooks, and a small cassette recorder. I wouldn't have bothered to report it but there was a police station just yards away, so I went in and gave my details, assuming that would be the last I'd ever hear of it. They called me the following morning and said someone had handed it in, obviously minus anything that seemed valuable.

I went into the station to pick it up, at which point I was asked, not told, to sit in an interview room. Two police officers came in — a caricatured good cop/bad cop duo. They told me they'd found a flick-knife in the case, and asked if it was mine. It was — a joke gift that a friend had given me from his vacation in Spain, where they weren't illegal, but they were in Britain. I hadn't taken it out of my bag yet and intended to use it as a letter opener. It was blunt and hardly worked; the bag would have been a better weapon. Even so, the older cop (bad) threatened to charge me, to put me in a cell, and God knew what else. The younger cop (good) reassured me, said his colleague was being too tough, and that if I just told him who had "supplied" me, they'd let me go. I felt like laughing at how ridiculous all this was, but that wouldn't have been the correct response at all.

Suddenly an alarm went off in the station and both good and bad cop ran out of the room. I waited, having no idea what to do, and after fifteen minutes walked out to the front desk, told a very pleasant policewoman what had happened, and asked what I should do. "Oh, just go home," she said. "Those two are a pair of twats who watch too much telly."

I fought the law, and the law didn't win.

Stolen bags and useless blades aside, I couldn't see how I could continue attending classes to study how to be a journalist when I was starting to be a working journalist with genuine demands on my time. I'd no idea how quickly John Pilger would want me to start and how much work would be involved. I had to be ready. I tried my best to combine attending classes with researching and writing articles, but when John told me more about the television show he was planning, it was obvious that I wouldn't be able to maintain the double life. I told the head of department at City that I wouldn't be back for the following semester, and he was understanding. He certainly didn't say that I would never work in this town again. As it was London, that would have been a bit of a problem.

The television show was to be called *The Outsiders*, a series of interviews conducted by John, with research done by me. I would also write some of the script and provide questions. It was planned to air in 1983 on the new Channel 4. There had been only three television services in Britain before this: BBC1, BBC2, and ITV. The Broadcasting Act 1980 began the process of adding a fourth, and Channel 4 started broadcasting in November 1982. That meant we were one of the first shows commissioned.

The interviews were with people from "outside" the system or establishment, and also people for whom John and I had a particular admiration. Sean MacBride — former chief of staff of the Irish Republican Army, lawyer, and co-founder of Amnesty International — was one of the guests. We also had Martha Gellhorn, the war correspondent and author of several books; someone who had lived through the Spanish Civil War and American Depression and was also once married to Ernest Hemingway. Wilfred Burchett was less well known. He was the first Western journalist to enter Hiroshima after the atomic bombing, and someone who had tried to report on the wars in Korea and Vietnam from a less Western point of view.

Salman Rushdie was also on the show. This was before the fatwa and the terrible attacks on him, and he was famous then for his superlative novel *Midnight's Children*, about India's move from colonial rule to independence. It won the Booker Prize, the James Tait Black Memorial Prize, and later the "Booker of Bookers" prize. Rushdie was charming and modest, and his life was so different from what it would become.

For a while, we had the same publisher, Jonathan Cape. I once took a girlfriend to Cape's Christmas party. Rushdie was there, but given he was one of the great young men of literature, I didn't approach him, even though we'd worked on a television show together. Suddenly, I felt a tap on my shoulder and there was Salman. "What's the matter, Michael — too important for me now?" It was a delightful thing to do and say to a twenty-two-year-old unknown like me. And my date for the night was more impressed than I can say.

Another guest was Jessica Mitford, who was a delight. She was warm, funny, and fascinating. She was one of the six famous and, in some cases, infamous Mitford siblings, who were renowned for their political differences. One of Jessica's sisters, Diana, married British fascist leader Oswald Mosley, and the two of them were interned for much of the Second World War. Another, Unity, was an appalling figure who adored Hitler, spent a great deal of time in Berlin, and enjoyed watching the private and public humiliation of Jews. Nancy was a gifted novelist, author of *Love in a Cold Climate*; Deborah married the Duke of Devonshire. Jessica, known as Decca, was a communist. Her first husband, Esmond Romilly, was killed in the Second World War, and her second husband, the American civil rights lawyer Robert Treuhaft, was Jewish. She and her husband refused to testify in front of the House Un-American Activities Committee, part of the anti-communist witch hunt, and she told me she was genuinely frightened that the family would be arrested and sent to some sort of camp. "The children became very excited," she said, laughing. "They thought they were all going to summer camp. But it was a terrifying time — terrifying."

She still had a refined English accent but said that when she went to see her sisters, they would say, "Darling, we can't understand a word you're saying." She also told us about when a U.S. serviceman home on leave tried to rape her. We were horrified. She broke the tension by explaining, "I started to recite the *Communist Manifesto* to him. I tried to bore him un-stiff." She laughed, so we laughed. Jessica wrote two timeless books, *Hons and Rebels*, about her family and her early years, and *The American Way of Death*, covering how the funeral industry was exploiting poor Americans.

Helen Suzman was equally lovely, maternal and approachable, but not as cuttingly funny as Jessica Mitford. Then again, few were.

She was a South African MP, a long-time opponent of apartheid, and for much of her career was the only member of the South African parliament to loudly oppose the country's racist policies. Hers was for many years a lone voice, at least in the country itself and in the political mainstream. Her liberalism and humanity shone through the interview. I asked her if she was ever scared. "Oh, yes," she said. "There was a time when people were falling out of windows, having accidents. In other words, they were being assassinated for being dissidents. Yes, it was frightening. Being Jewish increased the hatred. I remember other MPs shouting at me, 'Go back to Israel,' but then Israel became more military, built a relationship with South Africa, and it became too good for me. They stopped shouting it. Life is so strange sometimes." She was twice nominated for the Nobel Peace Prize.

The show didn't always run smoothly. Martha Gellhorn, Hemingway's third wife, was nervous and a little cold, and absolutely refused to discuss Hemingway. It was understandable that she wanted, quite rightly, to be known as an author in her own right, but to totally ignore her relationship with one of the most important novelists of the twentieth century seemed odd, to us and to the viewers.

Sean MacBride, the Irish politician, was fascinating but had obviously enjoyed the hospitality on the plane over from France, where he lived, just a little more than was absolutely necessary.

Later, we would conduct another interview, not for television, with Ken Livingstone, then mayor of London and controversial for his committed socialist views and policies. Mitford, Suzman, Burchett, MacBride, and others are dead now, but Rushdie and Livingstone remain important cultural and political figures.

The show aired on Sunday afternoons, hardly a prime spot, and production resources were limited, as was the audience. Still, it was important in its content and, on a personal level, allowed me to meet a group of deeply significant and often inspiring figures and gain a lot of experience in television. There was my name on the television screen, and the connection with John gave me a level of prestige that I hardly deserved.

John and I worked on some other projects together, but we weren't always politically aligned. I found some of his left-wing views too sweeping and absolute, and I had a dreadful relationship with one of his producers. Not with John, though, who was always supportive and giving. At eighty-four years old, when he passed away, he was still as vocal and determined as ever, and his is a voice that has been vitally important for decades.

*The Outsiders* didn't make me wealthy, but it did provide me with a steady income for more than a year. I decided to move out of my parents' house and buy my own, very small apartment in the centre of London. It was a tiny, thirteen-by-fourteen-foot single room in a block called Russell Court. It was adjacent to Russell Square in Bloomsbury, I could walk almost everywhere I needed to be, and while the sofa bed, miniature kitchen, and incredibly limited space were hardly luxurious, they were all mine — or at least, the mortgage was mine — and I was living on my own and in the very centre of London.

My writing for the *New Statesman* and work for Channel 4 were supplemented by some theatre and book reviews for the BBC World Service Radio, and I was just about able to pay the bills. It was what I'd wanted for some time, but I was surprised to find I wasn't especially happy. As I look back, I realize that my ambition had got in the way of my forming many lasting relationships, and there were times of genuine loneliness. Perhaps the search for a faith that would fulfill had never disappeared. Blaise Pascal said, "There is a God-shaped vacuum in the heart of each man which cannot be satisfied by any created thing but only by God the Creator, made known through Jesus Christ." All I knew was something was obviously missing, and I wasn't certain what it was.

# CHAPTER THREE

## MAN ABOUT TOWN

In 1982, one of my magazine interviews was with the movie producer David Puttnam, whose 1981 film *Chariots of Fire* had been nominated for seven Academy Awards and won four, including for best picture, best original score, and best screenplay. The movie is based on the true story of two British athletes in the 1924 Olympic Games. Eric Liddell was a devout Scottish Christian who refused to compete on the Sabbath, and thus gave up the chance of the gold medal he was likely to win. He eventually won another in the four hundred metres. The second athlete was Harold Abrahams, who was Jewish and faced an anti-Semitism that was far from uncommon at the time. He won the hundred-metre gold medal. It was a natural story, highly filmic, and caught both a British and Hollywood wave.

It was written by the actor and screenwriter Colin Welland, and I spoke to him for some background material on Puttnam for my interview. Colin was a well-known personality in Britain, who had appeared in the groundbreaking television police drama *Z-Cars*, and then in various other television shows and movies. His role in the film *Straw Dogs* led to a life-long friendship with Dustin Hoffman. But it was as a writer that he achieved the most. He wrote *Yanks*, starring Richard Gere and Vanessa Redgrave, and *Twice in a Lifetime*, starring Gene Hackman and Ellen Burstyn, and co-wrote other movies. He also wrote television dramas and stage plays. *Chariots of Fire* won him all sorts of awards, including a coveted Oscar. When he won it, he told the audience and the millions watching at home, "The British are coming!"

Colin was in many ways a much misunderstood man. Born in the north of England and raised in the small Lancashire town of Newton-le-Willows, he held on to his Northern and working-class identity with a public determination. That led to accusations that he was a "professional Northerner" — someone who parades his non-London persona around, almost artificially. That wasn't my experience with him at all. I'd met with Colin only to ask about his producer, David Puttnam, on *Chariots of Fire*, but our "quick lunch" became a three-hour session in which we laughed a lot, discussed his beloved rugby league, and argued about history and politics. In other words, we got on. He asked me along to watch the Fulham Rugby League team play. Rugby League was a professional, largely Northern breakaway from Rugby Union. The reason for the split was that working-class men, often coalminers or steelworkers, wanted a small amount of compensation for playing. The London-based, mostly middle- and upper-class administrators of the sport thought this heresy. Thus the division, with a few small rule changes. Colin was one of the people instrumental in bringing the essentially Northern game to London, and it was here that I saw him in his element.

A few days later, he told me about his next movie, a biopic about Robert Stephenson, who designed and built the Rocket — not the first steam locomotive but the first to bring all the various ideas and plans for the steam train together in one successful vehicle. That was as early as 1829, and it's a fascinating story. Colin had spoken to Sean Connery about playing the title role, movie studios had given their approval, and Colin asked me if I'd be his producer on the project. It would mean reading lots of books on the subject, visiting historically relevant places, and being the facts and figures person. I met with Colin and his agent to sign the contract and was officially employed to research the screenplay for a major movie.

For the next few months, I travelled alone to carry out research as well as accompanying Colin to various destinations concerned with the story. I met with experts in engineering and early nineteenth-century history and fell in love with the era and the theme. Colin took me to parties where I met genuinely famous actors and was not supposed to be impressed by them. That was impossible.

I heard him tell them the same joke several times, and it always got a laugh. "I was at an amateur Rugby League match back home and suddenly the ref blew the whistle as a funeral cortège passed by. He asked all the players to stand in respectful silence until the procession had moved through. Then he blew the whistle again and the game went on. When the match ended, I went onto the pitch and told the ref how impressed I'd been by what he'd done. 'Oh, it was the least I could do, really,' he said. 'After all, we'd been married for thirty-five years.'" It never failed.

Because Colin had won an Oscar, actors and directors from the U.S. were usually unaware of his position slightly outside of the British mainstream. British film and TV people were different from those in the U.S. Colin had his circle of friends, but I more than once witnessed a coldness bordering on disdain, and Colin was always hurt when he was not included in the list of the good and great for his theatre and TV writing. But, as he said to me once, "the money from movies helps me feel better."

After all the work, the travel, and the writing, the movie *Rocket* was never made. Colin was paid a huge amount of money for writing the screenplay but movies, even at that level, often never make it past the planning and writing stage. Stephen Fry wrote a script for a remake of *The Dam Busters* some years ago, with Peter Jackson — responsible for *The Lord of the Rings* franchise — set to direct. It sounded so exciting, but the film might never be made.

Colin and I remained friends, but after *Rocket,* he was asked to adapt Ralph Hurne's 1973 novel *The Yellow Jersey* into a film, and a researcher wasn't required. The story is about an English professional cyclist who comes out of retirement to help a star rider at the Tour de France. There are doping scandals, complicated love stories, action, and young men on bikes. What could be better box office? It was perfect for Colin. Carl Foreman was brought on as the producer, Colin's friend Dustin Hoffman was to star, and a huge commercial success was anticipated. That was the last I heard of it.

After *Rocket*, I did some work for Colin, about a young man whom the medical profession had written off after a terrible accident that left him in a coma. His family rejected the doctors' advice and nursed him back to health. The working title was *Lazarus*.

Colin died in 2015, after living with Alzheimer's disease for several years. He was eighty-one. I still remember when he met the woman I'd eventually marry; he went into his study to take his Oscar down from the shelf so she could pose with it for a photograph. He had a temper, he could be bombastic, but he was a good man who tried to stand up for those he saw as underdogs.

◻

While my brief not-quite-a-movie-career was happening, I'd taken another dive into organized religion. I was still writing for various magazines and newspapers and one of them asked me to interview Lord Longford. Francis Aungier Pakenham, Seventh Earl of Longford, First Baron Pakenham, Baron Pakenham of Cowley, KG, PC, was an author, former cabinet minister, campaigner, high-profile Roman Catholic, and a figure much loved, much mocked, and even much hated in Britain. In his long life — he would die in 2001, aged ninety-five — he served in Labour governments between 1947 and 1968, wrote political biographies of his friends Presidents Kennedy and Nixon and books of Christian apologetics, but he was best known as a social activist and campaigner for people often forgotten.

He was in many ways a social conservative who led crusades against pornography, declining morals, and abortion. But he was also a political radical, calling for the release from prison of some of the country's most detested and infamous convicts. He opposed the death penalty and advocated for shorter prison sentences and a greater concentration on rehabilitation. It was Catholicism, however, that was the essence of his life. Every thought and action was informed by a deep sense of commitment to the teachings of Jesus Christ and the authority of Rome. "I'm a Catholic," he once said to me, "because otherwise nothing makes any sense." Yet he was also regarded as an eccentric and wasn't always taken seriously. He was extremely tall and slim, with tufts of hair at the side of his head and a most extraordinary ability to look untidy.

There were those who couldn't forgive him for his championing of Myra Hindley. She was one of the Moors Murderers, a couple who kidnapped children and tortured them to death. They tape-recorded the screams of their victims. It led hardened policemen to break down in tears in the courtroom. Frank decided that Hindley had been cajoled by her lover into these devilish crimes and that after decades in prison, she should be released. The British public, and successive governments, guaranteed that this would never happen — echoes, of course, of Karla Homolka in Canada, but with a different outcome. For claiming that even the vilest criminal might be capable of change, and might have been part victim herself, Frank Longford was vilified in the media and even physically attacked. Far from silencing him, however, the vitriol seemed to make him stronger.

Similarly, in his campaign against pornography, he was mocked as "Lord Porn," and editorials and cartoonists had endless fun with his supposed enjoyment of, or obsession with, the stuff. In fact, he was a married man with eight children and had a very healthy and normal sex life. He simply thought it damnable to depict men and, particularly, women as pieces of meat for the titillation of the needy and the profit of the unscrupulous. He led a government commission on pornography and, as such, had to watch hours and hours of material. I once asked him if it had any effect. "Yes," he said, smiling ironically. "It always made me rather bored, sorry, and tired. But I had to admire the stamina of those young people."

He also called for a greater civility in society, more balance in the media, and a more equal distribution of wealth. He helped establish clubs and centres for very tough and damaged inner-city kids.

There was something abundantly charming about seeing Frank, in crumpled suit and crested tie, chatting with steel-hard young men about their former lives as soccer hooligans or street thugs. He never patronized, and always listened. He was also at the forefronts of the anti-racist movement as well as the pro-life community. For him, a belief in the sanctity of life included all humanity, at every stage of development. "I cannot oppose abortion unless I can be there helping that poor, single pregnant woman find a home and a job and support," he said once, over one of our long lunches. "Otherwise, I'd be a hypocrite. Can't be that. Just can't be that."

I might not have agreed with all his views, but I always admired him. I don't think he'd be at all comfortable with the modern anti-abortion movement.

Frank took an interest in me when we discussed his faith and when I questioned him about how he dealt with some of the more difficult issues of the day. He suddenly asked, "And you, Michael — have you ever considered the Roman Catholic Church?"

I replied, taken aback, that I had but I didn't think now was the time.

"Oh, dear boy, it never is. Let's go to mass together tomorrow morning."

We met outside St. James's Church in Marylebone, in central London, and went on to Spanish Place — a large, imposing Gothic structure. Inside the church it's quite dark, and everything I assumed a Catholic church would be like, and unlike what so many recent and modern Catholic churches actually are. Spanish Place was known as such because of its historic connections to the Spanish embassy when Catholic services were banned. This was because after the English Reformation in the sixteenth century, Catholicism was seen increasingly as a foreign, alien threat to England and its church. It would take until the nineteenth century for equality and tolerance to be achieved, and even then it wasn't accepted by everyone.

Frank guided me to a seat, rather than a pew, in front of a side altar, and seemingly out of nowhere, a ceremony began. I'd been to mass at university, but this was much grander and far more beautiful than anything I'd previously encountered. It was fairly short, as it was a morning service, largely for people to attend before they began work.

"Have a word with the priest in charge here, Monsignor Miles, and see how it goes," said Frank. "I won't bother you but if you do go ahead, do come into the church, I'd be honoured to be your sponsor — your godfather. If I could do it for Malcolm Muggeridge, I can do it for you," referring to the famous author, journalist, and television personality. At that, he shuffled off into the light and the street and the world that seemed so transient and flimsy compared with the beauty I'd just witnessed.

I did indeed see the priest, who turned out to be a lovable and deeply wise man who would instruct me in the Catholic faith for the next year, and then baptize and confirm me. I remember when I told my father what was happening. "If it makes you happy, fine. But don't talk to me any more about it," he said. Which, all things considered, wasn't bad at all.

When I was eventually received into the Church, a handful of friends were with me, and Frank Longford dutifully came along — we did in the end have fairly regular lunches during the period of instruction. He was my co-sponsor, along with Paul Goodman, still a close friend. Paul was Jewish, had converted to Catholicism a few years earlier, and was a leader of the Conservative student movement. He would become a writer for the *Daily Telegraph*; a monk for two years at Quarr Abbey on the Isle of Wight, where I visited him; and then a Tory MP. A circuitous and colourful journey. He's now the editor of *Conservative Home*, an influential media platform that probably gives Paul far more say in Conservative politics than he would ever have had as an MP. When he left Parliament, he said that it had become a place where "professional politics predominates, entrenching and empowering a taxpayer-dependent political class distinct and separate from those who elect them ... for better or worse, this future Commons isn't for me." It was a deeply principled decision, especially as he was likely to have held the seat for as long as he wanted it. But principled decisions from Paul are entirely typical.

The night of my baptism, I shook like a frightened child. I was in my early twenties, a grown man, but I felt so young and so weirdly vulnerable. I knelt in front of the huge, beautiful altar and felt something I could never then and can't now properly put into words. The gentle but powerful touch of Jesus, the reassuring coat of certainty put around my shoulders, a relationship with God dressing my naked soul. I know that the emotions of a great occasion can change the way we feel and are more the stuff of brain chemistry than a lasting and meaningful experience, but I'm convinced this was more than that. Something transformative happened, and I felt drawn through a gate of longing into a garden of grace. The opportunity I was given was magnificent but, in my weakness, I didn't do the work that was necessary for conversion to take flesh and to grow and mature.

Three days after my baptism, I recall lying on the sofa in my apartment and feeling driven to go out into the street and tell people all about faith and God. "I have to tell someone — I have to tell someone." I didn't, though. Of course I didn't. After all, I was me.

It was the first time I'd felt what I'm sure was the Holy Spirit. It's happened since, although not as often as I'd like. I know that some will doubt me and even consider this ridiculous. It was, they'll claim, not more than an extended serotonin rush, a feeling, something that can be entirely explained by the rational mind — nothing to do with God. I know what all of those feel like and this was different. So, we'll have to agree to disagree.

Then why didn't it stick? As I say, I was too complacent about it all. Reading a book about dieting won't make you lose weight. You have to actually diet. I took my Catholicism seriously, but I've often wondered if I was seduced by the cosmetics of it all instead of the deeper relationship with Christ that must be at the centre of a genuine Christian commitment. I'd been given that free of charge on that sparkling night, but I'd failed it. Perhaps I'd fallen for the aesthetics of it all, for the intellectual tradition of Evelyn Waugh, Hilaire Belloc, G.K. Chesterton, and that whole English Catholic literary heritage rather than going deeper and further. I tried to believe, I attended mass most days, but it was a flesh wound in my materialistic life, not a mortal shot. I was still the man standing on the beach who hadn't yet been soaked by those waves. I wasn't floating.

It was nobody's fault but my own, and those close to me tried their best. Frank took me to the Tablet Table, a rather grand meal held by the weekly Catholic magazine *The Tablet*. Founded in 1840, it was on the progressive wing of the church, was read far beyond the Roman Catholic community in England, and many eminent writers and politicians have contributed to it. Frank introduced me to the editor, who within a few days telephoned me to ask if I'd be interested in writing a television review column for them every two weeks. The job lasted less than a year, and apparently someone was displeased with me for criticizing King Juan Carlos of Spain who, in a TV documentary about his daily life, had made some flimsy comments about the Basques and their campaign for separation. I hadn't meant to be rude in any way — I was just being a TV critic, which I'd assumed was my role. I was told that this wasn't the end of my relationship with the magazine, but I knew that it was.

By 1983, I was writing for *City Limits*, a weekly London arts magazine. My work involved regular theatre reviews, and the main drama critic there, Jim Hiley, became a friend and mentor. He'd been asked to write the centenary book of the Theatre Royal Stratford East, which began its life in 1884. He was too busy working on other projects but told the theatre that he had a young friend — me — whom he thought would be right for the job. It was a staggeringly selfless thing to do. I went to the east London theatre, met with the director and staff, and they telephoned me later in the week to say they'd like me to proceed.

Finding a book publisher when you're twenty-four years old and unpublished isn't easy, and this was a commission involving a significant cultural landmark. For twenty years, between the early 1950s and the mid-1970s, Stratford East was home to Joan Littlewood's theatre workshop. This gifted director and teacher worked with her partner, Gerry Raffles, to introduce a new, grittier, more working-class form of drama to British theatre. With plays such as *A Taste of Honey* and *Oh, What a Lovely War!*, the theatre forced itself into the country's culture and conscience. Many of the regular actors became household names, and Richard Harris, Barbara Windsor, and Harry H. Corbett, among others, got their breaks there. Not Michael Caine, though — the irascible Littlewood told him to "Piss off to Shaftesbury Avenue [the West End]. You will only ever be a star." Her notes about him were still in the theatre records.

Even with Stratford East's reputation, I was turned down by three houses. Not the fourth, however. Quartet Books came to my rescue. They were a fairly small publishing house established in 1972 and acquired by Naim Attallah in 1976. Naim was a Palestinian Christian entrepreneur with an interest in literature and letters. He was ebullient and affectionate and was once described by the *Guardian* as a "legendary adorer of beautiful women." There were certainly a number of them around at Quartet, and when Naim agreed to publish my book, he told me my editor would be a young woman he'd hired by the name of Nigella Lawson. I'd no idea that she'd go on to become an internationally famous food writer and television presenter. I think we once shared a sandwich, but we bought it from the corner store.

The book was published in 1984 and widely reviewed. There was a stinker in the *Observer*, but most critics were fairly kind. I don't think it sold many copies and probably didn't deserve to, but it's still around electronically and people do buy it. The point was that I was a published author. Naim also agreed to publish *The Outsiders*, the book of the TV series presented by John Pilger. I wrote essays about each of the subjects, followed by transcripts of the interviews. It was published in 1985, which meant that I had two books in print by the time I was twenty-six. I also sold my miniature home in Russell Square and found a slightly less miniature one on Great Titchfield Street, which is a W1 address, meaning it couldn't be more central. It was on the top floor of a four-storey building, with no elevator or, for that matter, central heating. The main room was a little larger than the Russell Square doll's house, and there was a decently sized kitchen. It was still small — still a studio with a sofa bed — but much better than what I'd had. I paid around fifty thousand dollars for it and would sell it two years later for sixty thousand. Today it would go for well over a million dollars, and because of its location — a five-minute walk from the BBC and ten minutes from Oxford Street — I could rent it out for a small fortune. I weep myself to sleep most nights.

Because of London's size and activity, two free magazines were distributed at Underground stops throughout the city. Enormous numbers of these glossy-covered publications were given out, mostly full of ads. They made a lot of money, and combined pages of commercials with editorial content. One of them, *Girl About Town*, had heard of me through my book on the Theatre Royal and offered me a weekly theatre column. It was hardly the *Guardian* or the *Times,* but it paid well and meant I received free tickets for the theatre two or three times a week. I saw some extraordinary productions, and some awful ones.

For all its commercialism and strange title, the magazine was read by a lot of people. My column was popular, and I was asked to write some movie reviews as well, and also interview celebrities for a second regular column. I wrote profiles of Judi Dench, Anthony Hopkins, Emma Thompson, Rowan Atkinson, William Goldman, Jenny Agutter, Antony Sher, and dozens of others. An actress whom I won't name once threw a glass of wine over me at a first-night party because of something I'd written about her. I was only quoting someone else's opinion, but I probably deserved it.

The first year of my journalistic career, and the last year of my curly hair and thirty-two-inch waist.

That incident was highly unusual; most of the people I met were a pleasure. Judi Dench began the conversation by rubbing my hands because I'd walked to the interview without gloves, and it was cold outside.

Anthony Hopkins was seductively honest. I asked him if he'd ever been in anything he wasn't proud of. "I'm an actor, it's what I do, what I am, so I do my best in whatever I'm asked to do," he explained in that voice, difficult to resist even reading a dictionary. Then, suddenly, "No, I tell a lie. *Hollywood Wives*. Total rubbish. Did it just for the money."

I asked him about his alcoholism, as he'd been sober for some time.

"It's an illusion, you see — a great lie. When you drink, you think you're always the most interesting person at the party, the most clever and witty one at the dinner, you know. You're not, of course. Not at all. Others know it — you don't." He then paused. "Instead of passing out, I now fall asleep. Instead of coming to, I now wake up. That's the difference."

When the interview was published, he telephoned me to thank me, which means he must have made the effort to track down my number.

I also wrote about theatre for *Plays and Players* magazine and was asked to interview Hayley Mills, who had been a child actress in dozens of movies, was part of the Mills acting clan, and was now making something of a comeback as an adult actress. What the magazine's editor didn't know was that as a child, I had had an infantile crush on her, entirely innocent at the age of six or seven but, as the song says, the first cut is the deepest. We met at Joe Allen restaurant in Covent Garden, and she was lovely. As we were leaving the restaurant, I told her about my unrequited love.

"Oh, darling," she said, "almost every man I meet of your age tells me the same thing," and she laughed out loud and then hugged me. I'd no idea I had so many rivals.

I was also given the task of interviewing the actor Kenneth Griffith, who had appeared in more than eighty films between the 1940s and 1980s. He was one of those actors whom everybody recognized but not everybody could name. I arrived at his large home in Islington, and this fiery Welshman opened the door wearing nothing but a dressing gown. "Don't worry," he said in a loud Pembrokeshire accent, "I'm a notorious heterosexual."

He was. Married and divorced three times, involved in numerous relationships, the father of five children, he certainly did everything with a flamboyant passion. We got on and became good friends. I think he saw me as someone he could influence with his ideas. Not in any sinister way, but out of affection. It was flattering, because he was friends with some impressive people. He and Peter O'Toole were like brothers, would refer to each other by their surnames even when together because to them, it was paradoxically intimate. I'd sometimes listen to long, intense phone conversations with Ken sitting next to me and O'Toole's voice booming from the speaker. He'd been close to Peter Sellers, too, but always said that one of Sellers's partners had made the great comic actor end the friendship. I suppose I can see that having Peter Sellers and Griffith in the same room would leave very little space for anyone else.

He was a fine actor, but his genuine talents were frequently obscured by the roles he was given — occasionally splendid, but too often virtual caricatures. Frankly, he resented it. He always used the word "player" to describe his profession and thought — and I agreed — that he was as good as most, better than many. He also bridled at the censorship he faced over some of his documentaries. He adopted causes, and they were various, controversial, and even contradictory: the Boer War and the cause of the Afrikaners, Israel and Zionism, India, and Irish republicanism. He once told me that the only politician he viscerally hated was loyalist firebrand Ian Paisley. It was Ireland, and a documentary about Irish political and military leader Michael Collins, that led to a ban from ATV in 1973. It would take another twenty years for the BBC to air it. Ken would show people an enormous cigar in a glass box above the stairs and tell them, "It's the only bloody thing that Lew Grade ever gave me!" Grade ran ATV at the time.

But he could be foolishly provocative, too. "I kept describing her as a good wife," he told me of a young actress with whom he worked, emphasizing the word "good." The woman had told Ken she found the word patronizing, but that apparently only encouraged him.

Then he'd lament how roles became increasingly scarce as he entered his seventies. As we once strolled in St. James's Park together, he said, "You're honoured, mate. For years I couldn't come here because it was where I'd once go when I was rejected for acting roles. I'd sit on a bench and fall into depression."

He enjoyed nothing more than holding court, arguing his position, and delivering fierce monologues in character — I've seen him be Napoleon, Nehru, and Ben-Gurion in the middle of a crowded room, and everybody was glued to his performance. When in 1986 I told him I'd met a woman in Canada and was going out there to marry, he hugged me, kissed me on both cheeks, and said, "Be happy, you bastard — be happy." When he broke the hug, I saw there were tears in his eyes.

The editor of *Girl About Town*, where I wrote my theatre and interview column, was Louisa Saunders, still a trusted friend. Very much a woman of the left, she was eternally patient and kind, and helped me personally and professionally. She was always destined for greater things and has gone on to write for and edit several other magazines and newspapers. Through Louisa I met her sister, Kate Saunders, who in her twenties was an actress and appeared in television comedies and performed onstage. I once went up to Scotland to see her in a play at the Edinburgh Festival Fringe. She was by far the best thing in it. But it was as a writer and author that she truly excelled. Her children's books won prizes, she received magnificent reviews, and she was in great demand by publishers. But tragedy punched with a cruelty I've rarely seen. Her son took his own life when he was nineteen years old, her marriage ended, and then she was diagnosed with multiple sclerosis. She died of cancer in her home in 2023. She was sixty-two.

Kate had been with me when I was received into the Roman Catholic Church, and she herself was a strong Anglo-Catholic. The last time I saw her, with the MS obvious, she told me she'd lost her faith. She was resigned more than angry, and who can possibly blame her? I'm sure, however, that God never lost faith in her. This magnificent woman was like a figure from another age, a bright young thing with talent to burn, dominating dinner parties with humour and charm, and so full of humanity and strength. I still have a figurine I bought after we'd been to see the movie *Lady Jane*. "Darling," she said, "what utterly average performances." She meant, I think, that she would have been better, and she might well have been. Whenever I look at the little statue, I remember glorious Kate.

I was still writing for the *New Statesman* and also working shifts at their office, where I first met Francis Wheen, one of the most talented and gifted writers I know. Francis is two years older than me but was so much more worldly and literate. He was very close to Christopher Hitchens, who also worked at the *New Statesman* at the time but was hardly ever around. Francis would write a biography of Karl Marx that was translated into twenty languages and won numerous awards, including the Deutscher Memorial Prize, and several other books that are as erudite as they are perceptive. He became a regular broadcaster on BBC Radio and a regular guest of television quiz, news, and humour shows, and had columns in the *Evening Standard* and the *Guardian*. He was a mainstay at *Private Eye* magazine. Unfortunately, Francis would have to deal with severe back problems and chronic pain, which placed enormous limits on his ability to travel and work. If it hadn't been for that, I'm convinced his reputation would be even greater than it is. He's taught me a great deal over the years, made me laugh, made me think, and is one of the most Christian people I know, although I don't think he's a Christian.

While I was working at the *New Statesman* in 1983, I was asked to interview the children's author Roald Dahl. He was famous then, and famous even now, some years after his death. Netflix, for example, recently bought the rights to his children's books for an enormous amount of money. As well as controlling film and television productions, the company will produce stage shows, spin-off games and, for all we know, a Roald Dahl World where eager visitors will experience Charlie's chocolate factory, the Big Friendly Giant, or Matilda dancing with the witches. While the precise amount of the purchase hasn't been revealed, it must have been of giant-peach proportions, because in 2019 alone the Dahl estate earned fifty million dollars from the author's works.

Which is all very well for Dahl's family and fans, but not entirely reassuring for those of us who are familiar with his repugnant and clinical anti-Semitism. When the Netflix deal was made public, there were a few references to what Dahl had said about Jewish people, and the estate made a brief, conveniently timed, and not-easy-to-find apology on its website, but that was mostly it. That simply wasn't an adequate response, and I should know because I was the person who broke the story. Dahl had just reviewed the book *God Cried*, about the Israeli war in Lebanon, and his comments and his criticisms of Israel were extreme and jarringly sweeping. There seemed to be something visceral about his anger, something more personal and dark than anti-Zionism or empathy with the Palestinians. He'd written of "a race of people" — the Jews — who had "switched so rapidly from victims to barbarous murderers," and said the United States was "so utterly dominated by the great Jewish financial institutions" that "they dare not defy" Israel.

Even so, Dahl was eager to be interviewed, and I was the person chosen to speak to him. He was polite and not unfriendly. And entirely malicious. "There is a trait in the Jewish character that does provoke animosity — maybe it's a kind of lack of generosity toward non-Jews," he carefully explained. "I mean, there's always a reason why anti-anything crops up anywhere." Pause. "Even a stinker like Hitler didn't just pick on them for no reason."

It's always difficult to recall specific emotions, but I think I was confused rather than anything. Was this some sort of deep irony that was over my head, or a satire he was about to explode or explain? Nope. With little change in tone, and still courteous, he told me that during his service in the Second World War, he and his friends didn't see any Jewish men fighting, and he was about to say something else when I finally responded. Firmly but not rudely, I told him that my father was Jewish, that my grandfather had won all sorts of medals in North Africa and Europe, that Jews fought in enormous numbers in all of the Allied armies, were often over- rather than under-represented, and that this slimy canard of Jewish cowardice was beneath him. At which point he coughed, mumbled something about "sticking together," and then promptly ended the interview.

After the article appeared, I heard nothing from Dahl or his people, and in those days, before social media and twenty-four-hour news roared immediacy into daily life, his comments seemed to be largely forgotten. I was told that he might be senile or, most memorable of all, "just having a bad day." That bad day was a long one because seven years later, he gave another interview, not to me, in which he said, "I'm certainly anti-Israeli, and I've become anti-Semitic. ... It's the same old thing: We all know about Jews and the rest of it. There aren't any non-Jewish publishers anywhere — they control the media: jolly clever thing to do. That's why the president of the United States has to sell all this stuff to Israel."

There was never any apology from Dahl, clearly because he did not think there was anything to be sorry about. The paragraph of contrition on the official website took a very long time to come, and while my interview has been quoted every few years, Dahl's reputation has hardly been trashed. In a 2021 biopic of the man, *To Olivia*, Dahl was portrayed by Hugh Bonneville, best known for being kind and nice in *Downton Abbey*. The film is about the death of a child, and nobody was expecting the man to be marching around ranting at alien conspiracies, but it still stings. Dahl's works are undeniably impressive, and arguments about separation of creator and creation have raged for generations. What does continue to hurt, however, is the fact that he seems to have largely gotten away with it. We're not speaking of Wagner or Ezra Pound here, but authors and artists who have made far more ambiguous comments about race than Dahl, and ones often soaked in anachronism, are frequently given a much harder time than this nasty old anti-Semite.

It's facile and reductive to compare minority status as if it were a competition. Jews do matter, anti-Semitism isn't pervasive, and most critics of Israel certainly do make that vital distinction between objections to the policies of a nation-state and downright racism. Not Dahl, though, and he never even pretended otherwise. It's difficult but possible to deal with anti-Semitism expressed before the Holocaust, but from someone with full knowledge of the Shoah, it's a struggle, and one I'm not sure we should even attempt. Steven Spielberg directed *The BFG*; Taika Waititi, a self-described "Polynesian Jew," is working on a series based on the world of *Charlie and the Chocolate Factory* as part of the Netflix deal; and if I'm honest, I read Dahl's stories to our children when they were small. But always with a heavy heart. His words beyond his books will never entirely leave me.

The Dahl story brought me publicity and a greater profile, and I can only imagine what it would have done today. While I was walking back from an interview with a foreign news service about what Dahl had said, I met Sue, who worked close by. This was in Soho, a well-known red-light area of London, in those days full of shops that in the pre-internet age still sold pornographic magazines and videos. The streets were lined with ads for sex workers — Young Model Upstairs, etc. — and sometimes there would be a prostitute on each floor of the building. As I was walking home from the interview, a woman came out of the doorway, tripped, and fell flat on her face. I rushed to help her, steadied her, and asked if she was okay. She was shaken and bruised but otherwise fine. She'd caught her high heel on a loose step as she was leaving work to grab some lunch. The work was the usual for Soho. I held her arm a little self-consciously and took her to a nearby café, where I bought her a drink to steady herself.

"You're so kind," she said. "If you're interested later, I can offer you something in return for half the price, just to say thanks."

I said it was thoughtful of her but there was no need. It seemed to surprise her, as I suppose so many of her interactions with men were about anonymous sex. It wasn't that I was indifferent to her charm, more that I was too frightened of the whole thing. The result was that we chatted, and became acquaintances, if not friends. Once she realized that I found her interesting for herself, she began to trust me and was anxious to talk about what she did. She couldn't share it with anyone else, partly because she was putting her daughter through a private school and was determined to be regarded as "respectable" by the other parents.

She invested her money wisely, knew that her career had a limited time span, was studying accountancy for after retirement, and always voted Conservative. I've seldom met someone with such a calm and measured outlook on life, and while she never found out very much about her clients, even when they were regulars, she wasn't contemptuous of them and even had a genuine sympathy. There was one that she called "the fat boy," a very young man who was obese and came to see her every week. "The poor sod can't find anybody he doesn't have to pay. I'm doing a service, really — always try to make him feel happy."

She had a "maid," an older woman who greeted the men, made sure they weren't threatening or what she described as "not quite to be trusted," and who provided safety in numbers. "In ten years of this, I've only had one violent one. We managed to throw him out. We're careful about drunks, though. They're unpredictable."

We met twice more before she moved out of Soho. I once asked her if any well-known people came to see her. "I could never tell — that would be wrong," she said, smiling. Then she told me the name of an established BBC anchor, whom I later met at a friend's dinner party. I didn't discuss our mutual friend.

With two books published, I could approach new publishers with my resumé, some sort of proof that I could produce what was required. I'd developed an interest in the author and journalist G.K. Chesterton, and while Quartet Books made me an offer for a biography of the man, I shopped the proposal around to some larger houses. Jonathan Cape, which was extremely prestigious and the publishing home of some of the country's leading authors, surprised me by liking the idea. They paid more than Quartet and had far better distribution abilities and links to foreign publishers. I thanked Quartet but signed on with my new publisher, which would eventually be swallowed up by Random House.

Chesterton is a difficult and complex man. The author of the Father Brown stories, *The Man Who Was Thursday*, *The Napoleon of Notting Hill*, stylish and penetrating biographies, and volumes of journalism, he had a genuine cleverness and ability to charge through clutter and hypocrisy, like some grand knight of traditional values. His observations still seem highly relevant: "The Christian ideal has not been tried and found wanting. It has been found difficult; and left untried," he wrote. "A dead thing can go with the stream, but only a living thing can go against it," and "My attitude toward progress has passed from antagonism to boredom. I have long ceased to argue with people who prefer Thursday to Wednesday because it is Thursday."

Chesterton's gift — his charisma, if you like — was the ability to be a middleman of intellectual ideas and popular curiosity.

He could explain philosophy to the masses and mass to the educated atheist, could write weekly and sometimes daily newspaper columns, and then produce a biography of St. Francis or Charles Dickens that impressed life-long devotees. When he published his life of Thomas Aquinas, the world-renowned Thomist scholar Étienne Gilson was distraught. "For many years I have studied St. Thomas and written on him and now a journalist writes a better book about him than I have!"

Yet within Chesterton, within the style and the brilliance and the originality, there was something darker. Author and editor Richard Ingrams, an admirer, put it well when he wrote that he "shut his eyes to a great deal of the unpleasantness and cruelty in the world, including his own circle."

Ingrams was referring to Chesterton's comments about Jewish people — anti-Semitism being a subject that seldom seems to disappear in my journalistic career. This tension was at the epicentre of my book, and something I think I dealt with fairly. He was heavily influenced by his brother Cecil, a man of limited talent who was obsessed with what he saw as negative Jewish influence in media and finance. He led a vitriolic campaign against the handful of Jewish figures who were involved in the 1912 Marconi scandal, an early form of insider trading, mostly involving non-Jews. In addition, with the far more talented Hilaire Belloc, Cecil developed a virtual ideology based on the belief that Jews were alien to British society and a direct threat to its future.

Cecil died at the end of the First World War, through illness rather than combat, and shortly afterward, Chesterton wrote an open letter to Lord Reading (Rufus Isaacs, the first Jewish lord chief justice of England), as the politician was about to travel to Versailles as part of the British delegation to the peace conference. It's drenched in anti-Semitism, with references to "the Jewish international," "alien psychology," and "Daniel, son of Isaac, go in peace, but go."

But there is much more than letters written in grief, perhaps under the influence of friends. Chesterton may have been led farther along a dark path by those around him, but his mingling of misplaced medievalism, English insularity, and instinctive distrust of what he always offensively assumed to be Jewish characteristics led to his own brand of error and cruelty. Many, though far from all, of his contemporaries might have had prejudices about Jews, and sometimes expressed them, but Chesterton's frequent comments, his attacks, and then defence of his position or attempted justification single him out.

In his book *A Short History of England*, for example, Chesterton praised the expulsion of the Jews by Edward I as the actions of a "tender father of his people"; in his journalism, he condemned the British press for opposing the French military and establishment's anti-Semitism during the Dreyfus affair; and he even called for Jews to be forced to wear a form of public identification.

Then there were the clawing vulgarities. In *On Lying in Bed and Other Essays*: "I am fond of Jews/Jews are fond of money/Never mind of whose. I am fond of Jews/Oh, but when they lose/Damn it all, it's funny." And this from *The Flying Inn*: "Oh, I know a Doctor Gluck/And his nose it had a hook/And his attitudes were anything but Aryan;/So I gave him all the pork/That I had, upon a fork/Because I am myself a Vegetarian."

His defenders argue that he was a Zionist, but that's far too facile an analysis. While many at the time who supported the creation of a Jewish state did so because they thought it would lead to Jewish security and dignity, Chesterton was more concerned with what he was convinced was the foreign, un-English nature of the Jewish people. In other words: find them somewhere else to live. This was a natural, even inevitable, consequence of his obsession with what he referred to as "the Jewish question," making incessant references to "plutocrats" and "financiers" — a vocabulary that would soon become part of the litany of genocide.

The other common defence is that he was vehemently anti-Nazi. That's certainly true, though he also cheered for fascism elsewhere, especially when it was wrapped in Catholic nationalism. Chesterton wrote of thousands of Jews being "rabbled or ruined or driven from their homes" by the Nazis, who "beat and bully poor Jews in concentration camps," and how "I do indeed despise the Hitlerites." He died before the Holocaust was fully implemented, and with his authentic opposition to eugenics and his hatred of what he saw as "Prussian barbarity," he would likely have been disgusted. But opposition to mass murder and ethnic cleansing doesn't forgive someone of anti-Semitism, and those who help to create a climate where racist atrocity is permissible share a certain responsibility for its reality. While the claim might groan in its banality, he certainly did have Jewish friends whom he sincerely liked, and he was appalled by the idea of Jews being harmed because of who they were, but he also played a game of grimy hide-and-seek with the issue, popping up to provoke and condemn and then claiming innocence or, as his partisans would claim today, purity of intent. That just won't do.

I wrote, perhaps with far more sanguinity than was deserved, that when weighed in the balance, G.K. Chesterton may not have been completely on the wrong side of history, that at least he wasn't part of the problem, and that when the testing-time came, he saw the threat before others were aware. I'm not sure if I'd still say that. He may not have been the worst, he may well have changed his mind if he had lived longer, but the damage was done.

The Chesterton book wasn't to be published for a while, but word had spread that I was working on it, and because of that I was invited to a large conference about the man at St. Michael's College, University of Toronto. Chesterton died in 1936, so this was the fiftieth anniversary, meaning his works were out of copyright in some countries and it was time for a commemoration. I wasn't sure if I wanted to go. I'd never been to Canada, but it was a long flight, and I had another invitation to speak at the same time, one that was much closer to home. I opted for Toronto, which turned out to be the right decision.

I arrived in Toronto, where I was almost denied entry. My passport was slightly crumpled because I'd dropped it on the beach at the Dead Sea, of all places, and the chain-smoking woman in immigration doubted its authenticity. In a brilliant piece of questioning, she read my place of birth, Essex, and then said, "It's written here that you were born in Manchester." That's odd, I replied, because I thought it was Essex. I got the strong feeling that she didn't like me at all, but I suppose she needed a better reason to send me home than a creased passport.

I was greeted outside by a young man, my driver, who explained that he was a Basilian. That's a mostly Canadian order of Roman Catholic priests that I'd not heard of before. I thought he'd said he was a Brazilian. "I'm impressed," I said to him. "You've no accent at all." He very graciously told me I wasn't the first person to make that mistake. I think I was, though.

The conference lasted several days and featured academics, authors, and experts far more qualified than me, a mere journalist who was interested in Chesterton. The other difference was that I was twenty-seven years old, substantially younger than any of the other speakers. I looked different, too. There was a lot of tweed and corduroy around and here was me with an earring, unusual for men in Canada back then; aqua-green contact lenses; and what hair I still had heavily gelled. I wore a green suit. The very idea of it all now makes me want to hide.

My lecture was titled "The Marconi Scandal, G.K. Chesterton, and Edwardian Anti-Semitism" and seemed well received. For the rest of the conference I listened to other speakers, went to functions, walked around Toronto, and then attended an end-of-conference party. I was approached by an older man who seemed to be with a beautiful young woman with long, black hair, deep brown eyes, and olive skin. She had a shy loveliness, and I was smitten. The man praised my lecture and then the young woman, obviously nervous, said, "You're amazing." Assuming this would never happen again, I decided to marry her. And I was right, it hasn't ever happened again.

Her name was Bernadette and she seemed genuinely interested in me. I made a point of sitting myself next to her at dinner and for the final lecture, and then mumbled something about her showing me Toronto the following day. She was actually from Whitby, outside of the city, and hardly knew Toronto at all. But she agreed, we met, and then spent the rest of my time in Canada, three or four days, together. Leaving to return to Britain was difficult, but I had no choice. It would have been much easier today with Zoom, Facebook, and emails, but in 1986, it meant expensive phone calls and letters. I spoke to friends in Britain and asked their advice. They all said I should go out to Canada again and not waste any time.

I booked a cheap flight, spent two weeks with Bernadette, and met her friends and family, and then she visited me in London for Christmas. We'd met only in September but something about it all felt so solid and meaningful. Perhaps it was the novelty of a new country; perhaps I was for some reason disillusioned with Britain, or more likely with myself. Whatever the explanation, I was certainly facing some sort of crisis, a feeling that I had to try something new and challenging.

My journalism in Britain had begun to seem perfunctory, and after having met Bernadette, I was constantly distracted. I flew over to Canada every month or two, but the pain of the separations was difficult to tolerate. Surely it was far too early to make a commitment, and would I move to Canada or Bernie to Britain? She was a high school teacher and part of a very large family. It would be a sacrifice, whoever made the change, but I felt, perhaps naively or even arrogantly, that it would be easier for me.

On one of my trips to Toronto, I'd been introduced to a producer at the CBC called Louise Lore. She was quite senior and the woman in charge of a show called *Man Alive*. It fell under the religion department but was more a general interest show where a whole procession of people was profiled and discussed, and sometimes controversial and challenging subjects addressed. Arguably, it had its best days behind it, but was still innovative and popular. Louise Lore brought me in for an interview, we spoke about my work in Britain, and she explained that she needed to hire a new researcher who would also help with some scriptwriting. The interview went well, and she said she'd let me know.

I needed to know if I could make the move to Canada and have an income, so I pushed her to find out whether I'd got the job. I had. That was kind of her, and she would be a professional and understanding employer to work for. In the end I don't think I gave her my best, but there were circumstances around that. But I'd now found employment in Toronto if I wanted it, and this made my decision much easier. If Bernadette would have me, I'd emigrate.

When I write these words now, I realize how momentous and even irrational my decision was. I was successful in Britain and had good friends, loving parents, and security and familiarity. In a way, my decision is so very romantic; I might sound courageous, but I've thought for some time that I was immature and selfish. I've no regrets, Canada has been generous to me, and Bernie and I are still together thirty-seven years later, but I gave so little thought to what my move would mean for those around me, to those who loved me. None of them said anything negative because they wanted me to be happy, although one friend said, almost in passing, "You'll never return here to live, you know. This is it. You might think you can live in two places, maintain friendships, but you won't." He was partly right. I've managed to maintain friendships, if not to the extent that I would have liked. It was my parents I must have hurt the most, and they'd have been the last people to say anything critical about my decision.

At the heart of it all, despite any success I enjoyed in Britain, I wasn't especially happy. I'd wanted media success, wanted to live in the centre of London, wanted to go to fashionable parties, but once I'd achieved all of that, I was oddly unsatisfied. There was still an emptiness, almost a hunger for something different and new. It was childish of me to assume that a new country, even a wonderful wife, could repair any wounds I had, but that was my underlying belief.

Bernadette and I were married on July 4, 1987, just outside of Toronto, in a Roman Catholic church. My mother and Stephen Hayhurst, my oldest friend, were there. Not my father. He might not have been in any way religious, and his Jewishness was entirely cultural, but he still found it impossible to see his son married in a Catholic church. It seemed so alien to him. He never thought I'd be married in a synagogue, but this was too much. "If I saw all of that," he said, "I think I'd be sick." That was hard for me to take. But that was my father: loving, giving, often selfless, but sometimes so tough to understand.

After a day in Toronto, we flew out to Portugal to begin our honeymoon. We travelled from Lisbon to the Algarve, then to Spain, where the romance of Toledo, Seville, and the much under-appreciated Madrid delighted us. We caught a train to Lourdes, then spent some time in Paris before catching a boat to England for a few days in London, and finally flew back to Toronto. We drank endless amounts of staggeringly cheap and surprisingly good red wine, often from boxes. We dined on local food, walked for miles, sometimes slept on trains, and met welcoming and thoughtful people. I don't think we really knew each other that well when we got married and, in many ways, were irresponsible and rash to move so quickly. We were and still are extremely different people, with different senses of humour, some different interests and, to a certain degree, different outlooks on life. But we share a great deal, too, including a mutual devotion, a lasting romance, and the love of our children and now grandchild. The differences in our up-bringing, family background, and character have sometimes been an enormous challenge, but there's a love bond between us that always glues us together despite any disagreements or differences we have. The fact that we've been together so long proves that a marital partnership based on understanding, selflessness, love, care, and empathy, built around a solid commitment, can last whatever the obstacle. We've argued, we've had our issues, but the genuine marriage of souls and people that began in inchoate form back at the University of Toronto is stronger now than it ever was. It also helps that I know she's out of my league and that I'm a very fortunate man.

After the honeymoon, we were back to the pressures of reality. I had to get to know a country that was far more different from Britain than I had thought, had to make new contacts and friends, and learn how to live three thousand miles away from home. We had very little money, as I'd paid off Bernadette's student loan from my savings, and after we'd bought some furniture for our new apartment, things were financially challenging. My job at the CBC was in Toronto, but Bernadette's school was in Ajax.

I knew almost nothing about where we ought to live and agreed to rent a floor of a house in Oshawa, which is a city of which I've very few good memories. The daily commute meant a bus ride to one station, a train in to Toronto, then a subway ride to my office. It was far too much, especially with the erratic hours required of someone working in television. Sometimes I slept in the office in Toronto so as to avoid the commute. This was clearly never going to work.

I also had to finish the book on G.K. Chesterton, with a deadline fast approaching, so that whatever free time I had was taken up with completing the manuscript. I managed it, sent it off to Jonathan Cape in London, and tried to concentrate on my role at the CBC. Some of the shows I worked on were rewarding, others not. I co-wrote the script for an hour-long special called *Millennium — 1,000 years of Christianity in Ukraine*. It was directed by the very talented Halya Kuchmij, and something I enjoyed. It was my first exposure to Ukrainian history and culture, and we were both proud of what we'd achieved. But I was losing interest in my job, the commuting was exhausting and impractical, and at around two-thirds of my contract, we decided to part ways. The show's producers were totally justified, and I was relieved. Now, however, I'd have to replicate my freelance life from Britain. Apart from anything else, our first child was due; Daniel came along in September 1988. I was a husband, a father, and a freelance journalist in a new country. I had no real idea how to do any of them.

# CHAPTER FOUR

---

# THE BALD ONE FROM THE RADIO

Here I was, a stranger in a strange land. Not that strange because with a few variations, we spoke the same language, but words do not a nation make. Britain is a more tribal, more satirical, less kind culture than Canada. The similarities between the two countries are more cosmetic than people might think, but at heart there's still a thread of shared or semi-shared context and history that made everything much easier for me than it could have been. I've met too many immigrants from Africa, Asia, and Latin America to seriously believe that I had it tough when I came here. It was not as easy as I'd hoped, but that's something entirely different. I had to work to make a mark, and even to make a living. In those early days, we were filling up the car half-full with gas to save money, and paying off the phone bill in installments. Thank God that state of affairs didn't last, because it put a strain on our marriage.

My biography of G.K. Chesterton was published in 1989. The reviews were generally positive, with the late Bernard Levin in the

*Sunday Times* writing, "Of all the studies of G.K. I have read, this is the best, deepest, and most nearly complete." This was important, because Levin was regarded as one of the pre-eminent voices in highbrow British media. The *Toronto Star* described it far too enthusiastically as "the definitive work on Chesterton and one of the finest literary biographies in years." It didn't have much influence on sales, but it worked miracles on my reputation as a scholar. Which — and this is not false modesty — I'm not. I know scholars, have a son who is one, and that's not me.

We were still living in Oshawa, a town centred on the local, enormous car manufacturer. I'm from a working-class background but this was never a comfortable place for me to be. The local chain bookstore asked me, as an author living in the area, to sign and sell books in the shopping mall where it was situated. I sat there, books in front of me and pen in hand, for almost two hours as indifferent people walked past and either ignored me or regarded me as someone who had gone to the wrong store. I'm not sure I've ever felt more out of place. We sold no books, and of all the many book signings I've done over the years, this one will remain in my memory for all the wrong reasons.

There were a few hopeful signs. Paragon House bought the U.S. edition of the book, and it would over the years be republished by several other houses — my contract specified that, after a few years, the rights of my books reverted to me. Several of my earlier books, for example, have now come back into my ownership, and I gave the rights for some of them to an electronic publisher based in Britain. I receive a small amount every time one is purchased online and each year receive a royalty cheque, which is usually just big enough to buy us dinner at a fairly good restaurant. Being a Chesterton biographer means I still write about the man, because he often becomes newsworthy and remains a significant influence over modern writers, especially if they're conservative. He was, whatever his faults, a literary genius, and still has much to say to a deeply troubled world. When our first child, Daniel, was born in 1988, we gave him "Gilbert" as one of his middle names (poor sod), as Chesterton was Gilbert Keith and had indirectly brought us together and made Daniel possible. Dan has his mum's intellect, is a frighteningly deep thinker, and is now a professor of philosophy at a U.S. university. That — not me — is a scholar.

Because of the relative success of the Chesterton book, I pitched Jonathan Cape another idea, a life of H.G. Wells, with a very different take on the man from earlier biographers.

There's an anecdote about the author of *The Invisible Man*, *The War of the Worlds*, *The Time Machine*, and so many other bestselling books that rather exemplifies his character. At a London theatre in the 1920s, Wells was approached by a nervous, eager young fan. "Mr. Wells, you probably don't remember me," he said, holding out his hand. "Yes, I bloody do!" replied Wells, and rudely turned his back.

Personality aside, Wells also dabbled in anti-Semitism, racism, and social engineering, and in this atmosphere of instant outrage and fashionable iconoclasm, it's surprising that he hasn't been more targeted for symbolic removal. He hasn't been cancelled. Then again, perhaps it's not so surprising. Because while the undoubtedly gifted author said and believed some dreadful things, he was also a man of the left. And when it comes to cancel culture, socialism can often be the ultimate prophylactic. In other words, people of the left have sometimes got away with murder, even literally.

George Bernard Shaw said of Wells's nastiness and ugly views, "Multiply the total by ten; square the result. Raise it again to the millionth power and square it again; and you will still fall short of the truth about Wells — yet the worse he behaved the more he was indulged; and the more he was indulged the worse he behaved."

For much of the early twentieth century, eugenics was a creature of the left as much if not more than the right. Shaw himself, Sidney and Beatrice Webb, and many other left-wing intellectuals were convinced that for the lives of the majority to improve, there had to be a harsh control of the minority. Wells argued that the existing social and economic structure would collapse and a new order would emerge, led by "people throughout the world whose minds were adapted to the demands of the big-scale conditions of the new time … a naturally and informally organized educated class, an unprecedented sort of people." The "base," the class at the bottom of the scale, "people who had given evidence of a strong anti-social disposition," would be in trouble. "This thing, this euthanasia of the weak and the sensual, is possible. I have little or no doubt that in the future it will be planned and achieved." He wrote of "boys and girls and youth and maidens, full of zest and new life, full of an abundant joyful receptivity … helpers behind us in the struggle." Then, chillingly, "And for the rest, these swarms of black, and brown, and dirty-white, and yellow people, who do not come into the needs of efficiency … I take it they will have to go."

It's not clear where the Jews would come into this, but if Wells wasn't a professional anti-Semite, he was certainly a talented amateur. "I met a Jewish friend of mine the other day and he asked me, 'What is going to happen to the Jews?' I told him I had rather he had asked me a different question: What is going to happen to mankind? 'But my people —' he began. 'That,' said I, 'is exactly what is the matter with them.'"

And of the First World War, "Throughout those tragic and almost fruitless four years of war, the Jewish spokesmen were most elaborately and energetically demonstrating that they cared not a rap for the troubles and dangers of English, French, Germans, Russians, Americans, or of any other people but their own. They kept their eyes steadfastly upon the restoration of the Jews."

It was explained that the first volunteer for the American forces in Europe was Jewish, that there were numerous German Jewish winners of the Iron Cross, and that Jewish people died for every nation. Wells's response was sullen dismissal, then: "There was never a promise; they were never chosen; their distinctive observances, their Sabbath, their Passover, their queer calendar are mere traditional oddities of no present significance whatsoever." Leon Gelman, president of the Mizrachi Organization of America, responded, "H.G. Wells is brazenly spreading notorious lies about the Jews. His violent language betrays a streak of sadism that is revolting. If any man who professes to be an enlightened human being can preach such heinous distortions, then mankind is doomed to utter darkness."

Nor was Wells some fringe character. His books were international bestsellers, he had genuine influence, and when he met Stalin, the Soviet dictator and mass murderer was so impressed that he extended the interview. Nor did Wells's significance end with his death in 1946.

Jonathan Cape liked the idea and commissioned the book, putting in place the next couple of years of being an author. I was writing book reviews for newspapers and magazines in London, but in the late 1980s, this wasn't as technically straightforward as it is today. I needed more local work, so approached the two major dailies, the *Toronto Star* and the *Globe and Mail*, and arranged to meet with the book section editors. The man at the *Globe* was very strange and seemed far more concerned with talking about himself than about anything I could contribute to the paper. It was difficult to take him seriously, and there was clearly not going to be much, if any, work there. The *Star* was different. Ken Adachi, a gentle and soft-spoken man, gave me reviewing work immediately, and I would work as a critic for the *Star* for many years to come. Tragically, in 1989 Ken took his own life, after a second accusation of plagiarism. He was very helpful to me, and the news was devastating.

Suicide has been a distant fellow traveller in my life for some years now. The professor back at the University of Nottingham, who may have tried to recruit me into the British intelligence services, killed himself; three writers I knew also took their own lives; and one of my oldest friends did the same. It's a subject that concerns me deeply, and one now, as a priest, that I deal with relatively often. It's far more common than people think.

The friend who died by suicide was named Jimmy. I first met Jimmy when we were eleven-year-olds at school. He was the teenager I went to soccer games with, the young man I admired, then the adult who would cry like a baby when I telephoned him. He finally said his goodbyes and put an end to his suffering. I still miss him very much indeed, but I will never, ever blame him. I have no right to claim that judgmental ground; to do so would be not only arrogant, but also so uncaring and so horribly cruel. There was a time when I could never understand how life could be so painful that death would seem preferable. But we grow up, we learn, we mature, and we put away childish things. Jimmy seemed so accomplished to those who met him casually, so attractive and clever. But those of us who had seen the hidden gift that was Jimmy unwrapped saw the biting, sadistic depression at work, and knew of the endless struggles with medication, doctors, and therapy.

When he died, some of our mutual friends wrote to me in shock. He was, they said, so brilliant and funny and successful. Why didn't he think of the positive before giving in to the negative? I don't want to sound bitter, but that was such a callow, shallow misunderstanding of the all-embracing hell of depression. When the lights are turned off, there is nothing but darkness. The alternative to the pain is not less pain but no pain, and in the end the effort was simply too exhausting and the daily anguish too much to tolerate. In his final letter, Jimmy apologized for what he was about to do and asked forgiveness for any problems that he might cause.

When I heard about that, I wept. Kindness and concern for others even in the end times. But then those final moments are, they say, liberating and suddenly clean.

We can't fully understand suicide because such terror is by its nature beyond the understanding of the mentally healthy person. But anyone who has spent time with those experiencing it can gain at least a glimpse of the drowning mud that is mental illness.

I remember a neighbour in Toronto, such an innocent man, dented by paranoid schizophrenia, sitting in my home and physically moving his head in reaction to noises he was hearing that had not actually occurred. They were as real to him as were his hands or feet. He indeed has a beautiful mind, but life is not a movie. In many ways, mental illness is worse than most physical ailments. We know how to fix a broken limb or heal most diseases, but even when we know what obscures and scrambles the mind, we are often incapable of doing very much about it. A new generation of drugs has enabled psychiatrists and doctors, but they still fight the battle terribly under-armed.

Jimmy had tried everything, and he'd mentioned suicide before — even joked about it. He was raised Roman Catholic and knew that his church once believed suicide so heinous that it denied those who took their own lives a Christian burial. Chesterton, that man whose life I'd spent years covering, wrote, "Not only is suicide a sin, it is the sin. It is the ultimate and absolute evil, the refusal to take an interest in existence; the refusal to take the oath of loyalty to life. The man who kills a man, kills a man. The man who kills himself, kills all men. As far as he is concerned he wipes out the world." Such a crass interpretation of humanity and such a godless condemnation of those in agony is genuinely staggering.

Times, thank God, have changed — or are at least changing. But psychiatric care is shamefully underfunded, societal attitudes are still outdated, and outreach and empathy are progressing far too slowly. In the final analysis, what we can and must do as individuals is be present, listen, care, and love. Perhaps I am wrong to think and say this, but damn it, I was happy that there would be no more horror for my friend. I said it then and I say it now: rest in peace, my sweet boy. Rest.

I pray the same for Ken Adachi, whose death shook the Canadian literary world and those involved with the *Star*. But the books pages had to continue. I wrote a huge number of reviews for them.

One day, I sat waiting in the office for the then editor, the supportive and talented Susan Walker, to arrive. She'd ask me to select from the shelves what books I'd like to review. They were simpler days. Someone else came in, a tall and attractive man — a fellow Brit, I realized. His name was Paul William Roberts. As we began to chat, I realized we had a lot in common, and for some years, we were close friends. Paul had been at Oxford with Benazir Bhutto, Christopher Hitchens, and Martin Amis. Bhutto was to become prime minister of Pakistan, cruelly assassinated in 2007, and Paul had known her well. He was brilliant, handsome, fun, and terribly self-destructive. He taught me a lot about the Canadian literary scene; about how I could apply for government arts grants at federal, provincial, and municipal levels; and the people I should meet and know. He was connected and gifted, and if it hadn't been for the addictive and troubled side of his personality, I think he could have been a great and lasting talent. It was Paul who enabled us to move out of Oshawa and rent a three-bedroom, three-bathroom, air-conditioned apartment in a smart building just a few yards from the subway in west Toronto. Our rent was a mere six hundred dollars a month. He had friends who had friends in property, and we were the beneficiaries. It was life-changing in that it gave us space and a certain degree of luxury, and we were twenty minutes from the centre of the city.

Martin Amis came to town once for the Toronto International Festival of Authors, and he, Paul, Norman Sherry (the official biographer of Graham Greene), and I hopped from festival party to festival party. We drank heavily and I woke up at the home of someone I'd never met before. I apologized profusely, but was told that it was absolutely fine, that Martin Amis was charming, and was then offered a bacon-and-egg breakfast. Paul and I would eventually part ways, and as is so common in these things, I don't really know why. He moved to Quebec, and I'd heard that he had lost his sight. I tried to make contact with him but he never replied. He died, aged just sixty-nine, in 2019.

By the end of the 1980s, I was being offered work from all sorts of publications. My Wells book was provocative, detested by admirers of Wells but embraced by enough critics to satisfy my publishers. They asked for another book and I suggested a biography of Sir Arthur Conan Doyle, the creator of Sherlock Holmes. The *Globe and Mail* still hadn't offered me book reviews, but the newspaper's editor, William Thorsell, invited me in to see him and offered me a column. I remember that I was pretentiously wearing an Inverness cape, a huge and largely impractical garment that I'd had made. Thorsell graciously took my coat from my shoulders, sat me down, and asked if I'd like to write a men's column every two weeks. I'd never thought much about men as such and was certainly not involved in the men's movement or men's politics, but he gave me absolute freedom to write what I wanted, so I agreed.

The men's theme was broad and tenuous enough for me to write about issues that weren't directly pertinent to the brief. I wrote profiles of a loyalist paramilitary in Belfast, of a man who had been denied access to his children after an acrimonious divorce but one where there was no guilty party, a man making the case that he should have a say in his partner's decision to have an abortion, a trans woman — then a subject rarely, if ever, mentioned — and dozens of other issues. There were also much softer and more personal columns about men as fathers, husbands, and sons.

Within a year, editor Thorsell offered me a second column, to run in the arts pages. This meant that I'd be a weekly columnist in the paper, but the people in the arts department weren't at all happy. I'd heard, but can never know for certain, that there was visible anger from some of the senior people there, and their reaction wasn't entirely uncalled for.

By this time, I had a reputation as being a man of the right, a forthright conservative. The men's column had exposed certain gender issues that called for a second look at the place of men in contemporary society, and that didn't always go down well with everybody. Some of what I wrote in that column, and in my arts column, I would never dream of saying or believing today. But not all, and I'm still proud of much of what I wrote back then.

The other factor was that by now I'd started writing a satirical column for *Frank Magazine*, which was published out of Ottawa and intended to be something like Britain's *Private Eye*. I cherished the *Eye*, had friends working there, and am still linked to it. I'd written a few things for *Frank*, mainly gossip from the literary scene, and then suggested something that resembled Auberon Waugh's diary in *Private Eye*.

I knew and admired Auberon — known as Bron — the son of the great Evelyn Waugh. He wrote a funny, outrageous diary that, he said, was "specifically dedicated to telling lies." At its best, it held up a mirror to some of the absurdities that were becoming increasingly common in the public sphere. His diary persona wasn't him, and neither was mine, although some people in Canada simply didn't seem to grasp that. The *Ryerson Review of Journalism* described my *Frank* column as "written in a Swiftian vein." It continued, "Coren's alter ego, who savagely sends up the latest newsmakers, is that of a British upper-class intellectual stranded in the incomprehensible backwaters of Canada." That was about right.

I was hardly Jonathan Swift, but I was sometimes funny. I called it Aesthete's Diary and it was originally anonymous. I put my name to it later on, because I've never been comfortable with hiding one's identity. That's a major problem with social media. The target of the humour was supposed to be the author — the "aesthete"; it was clearly a fantasy, as he had a butler and lived in incalculable luxury. There was satire but there was also malice and cruelty. The powerful rather than the powerless were mocked, it was often cathartic and fun, but I was relieved when I made the decision to end it. Random House published a book collection of the diaries and it was my first bestseller, even if only for a single week.

Friends had told me that my standing as a columnist in mainstream media was being diminished, even damaged, by the Aesthete column. I don't know if that was true, but I'd run out of ideas and enthusiasm and after several years of writing it every two weeks, I gave it up. It's always best to quit on your own terms.

While I was writing my *Globe* columns, the *Financial Post* approached me and offered me a weekly column where I'd be allowed to write about whatever I wanted. They offered a good fee but added a syndication agreement in which I'd be paid a small amount every time the column appeared in other newspapers owned by the *Financial Post*. This brought the total to the highest I'd ever been paid for a weekly column. It wasn't an easy decision to leave the *Globe*, but when I telephoned William Thorsell to discuss it with him, he was gracious and told me I'd be foolish not to accept. I left the *Globe* on very good terms, at least with its editor.

The *Financial Post* column would continue for many years, and after yet another media group sale would morph into a weekly column for the Sun group, with papers in Toronto, Ottawa, Edmonton, Calgary, and Winnipeg.

The *Ryerson Review of Journalism* profile of me that I quoted earlier was in 1994. At the time, I thought it was unfair and unkind, but reading it again so many years later, I can see it's not as bad as I once thought. "During his seven years in Canada, Coren has written for the *Canadian Catholic Review*, the *Toronto Star*, the *Globe and Mail*, *Frank*, *Books in Canada*, *Quill and Quire*, *Saturday Night*, *Maclean's*, *Toronto Life*, numerous smaller publications, and a host of British newspapers. In addition, he's a contributing interviewer on TVOntario's *Imprint* and a once-a-week commentator on Toronto radio station CJRT-FM. Coren's reputation is that of a sharp-witted satirist, a brackish, bow-tie-sporting man who regularly assails Canadian political and journalistic heavyweights. But on this day in October, Coren has been demure, reserved-cherubic, even. Until, that is, I mention that a colleague has called him a 'literary prostitute.'"

I did object to the comment, because it was made by someone who came from a place of privilege that I'd never had. I took on work because I had to — I needed the money — and I enjoyed it. I'm a writer, writing is what I do, and while today I'm more selective and do sometimes turn work down, back then was a different and much less stable time. I was indeed writing for all sorts of people — not, however, very often for magazines. I was never very connected to the Canadian magazine world, which usually requires longer articles that I didn't have the time to work on. An exception was *Toronto Life*, which had asked me to write a handful of longer articles. There was a profile of Mike Myers, for which I was sent down to Los Angeles and where I first encountered sugar-free chocolate. I'd no idea it contained a substance that, eaten in high quantities, could act as a powerful laxative. I ate the delicious stuff in high quantities. Myers was a model interview, I was pleased with what I wrote, but I could write an entire essay about the washrooms at Universal Studios.

There was also a profile of a dominatrix who lived in the suburb of Richmond Hill. "What I really need," she said to me, "is a dungeon downtown." She gave me examples of essays her clients had written for her, where they'd listed their fantasies and scenarios. Most of them seemed to end with them being tied up and spanked. She'd cut off the top sections, which had their names and phone numbers, but on one of them the eager customer had written his name and number at the bottom. I considered contacting him to ask for an uncredited interview but was terrified I'd give the poor man a heart attack.

More controversial, though less leathery, was my interview with the Roman Catholic archbishop of Toronto, Aloysius Matthew Ambrozic. He was born in Dobrova, Slovenia; was a conservative; and had a reputation as a tough operator. The interview was in his office, with his secretary present, and most of it was fairly banal. He was guarded but not unfriendly. But then things took a different turn. When he died in 2011, the *Globe and Mail* wrote what I thought to be a very fair obituary.

> What had left Ambrozic "scorched" and deeply suspicious about the press was a 1993 *Toronto Life* profile written by the controversialist journalist Michael Coren. In it, Coren quoted Ambrozic as using the words "frigging" and "bitch" and calling the late Spanish dictator Francisco Franco "a conservative Roman Catholic and not a bad fellow." The Church circled its wagons around Ambrozic and Coren was deluged with hate mail. Though a faithful Catholic who struggled with printing the remarks, Coren stuck to his guns, saying Ambrozic had been "vulgar" in their talks, and he rebuked his co-faithful for expecting him to "lie."

The only error in the obituary was that the cleric's suspicion of the press predated me. He insisted on his own tape recorder being on throughout the meeting, which was something I'd never before encountered, in hundreds of interviews. At one point, when he was being particularly insensitive in his remarks, I even asked if he wanted me to turn my recorder off, and perhaps do the same with his. He said no, it was fine. I'd also been asked to submit my questions in advance, something else that has hardly ever happened to me. He proceeded to say things about a woman critic that were shocking from a priest, he was rude to those around him, and I was shocked at how bold he obviously thought he could be. I did try to be sympathetic to the man and sensitive to what he faced. I wrote, "This is one of those moments where Ambrozic indicates a form of weakness, even impotence. The truth is that he is a man who cares more about his church than anything else. He tries extremely hard but he cannot, in the long run, achieve its ends."

I struggled with the decision to write the article with all the comments included, and some of the things he said and did were never published. It was another journalist who persuaded me to include even what I did. "If a politician or a business leader or an actor had said all those things, would you have even a moment's hesitation?" She was absolutely right.

Years later, I was at a Christmas party at Conrad Black's house. Black, whom I've always liked despite some of his political views and occasional snipes at me, took me aside and said, without any mischief in mind, that the now cardinal was at the function. Conrad wanted to avoid embarrassment for either of us. There were lots of people at the party, but I was determined to apologize to the man for any pain I'd caused him, which I had also done in an earlier column. He may have said all the things I quoted, but surely we could move on. I finally got within yards of him as he was leaving. I tried to speak but have never seen a prince of the church move so quickly. He was out of the door and in his car before you could say "Nobody expects the Spanish Inquisition!"

It had an effect on my life as a Roman Catholic, which was fairly tenuous at that time, anyway. It all shook me hard: seeing how the archbishop behaved, how his Catholic supporters turned on me, how one priest bizarrely accused me of hanging around high schools to find out gossip about the archbishop (I've never sued anyone, but came close to it then), and the sheer lack of Christian justice involved. There were, mind you, other, more progressive Catholics who were glad of what I'd written and thought it was a long time coming. The fuss would eventually evaporate, as it almost always does, but only last year I heard a story being spread by an admittedly disgraced priest about my alleged refusal ever to try to speak to Ambrozic and seek peace between us.

□

Suicide entered my life again in 1994 in an acutely personal way. *Globe and Mail* arts journalist Stephen Godfrey had asked to interview me for a profile. I arrived at the small Toronto office I then rented on the morning of the proposed interview and saw that there were two messages on the answering machine. The first was from Stephen's wife, explaining that he was ill and wouldn't be able to make it. The second was from Stephen himself, saying that he was now okay and would be there. He arrived, interviewed me, and left. I have no memory of what we said, but I know it all seemed gentle and smooth.

On the Sunday night before the profile was to appear, I received a telephone call at home from the *Globe* arts editor, Katherine Ashenburg. She told me that my profile would be in the next day's paper, but I should know that the story of Stephen's death would be on the same page. I remember the emotion in her voice and realize now what a kind and brave gesture it was.

Stephen had been struggling with depression for a long time and ended his life in a cold ravine in Toronto. I've often wondered what I would have said if I'd had any idea of what Stephen was going through, and for a while I felt somehow guilty, as though I was somehow linked even distantly to the cause. Absurd but understandable. I was one of the final people to see him before his death. I hope I wasn't the last.

□

By this time, we'd left our rented apartment and bought our first house, a three-bedroom semi in central west Toronto. We'd sell it three years later and perform a minor miracle in that we managed to lose money in the city's property market. The timing was stormy perfection. We bought when the market was strong, sold when it was weak. I've never been good with money, never invested, and never looked for financial advice. The house loss would work itself out eventually because when we left that first property, we bought a huge, pre–First World War, wood-panelled home with an open fireplace, lots of rooms, a hidden staircase, two parking spots, a large garden, piles of atmosphere, all only a fifteen-minute walk from High Park. The children adored it, but it was in a rough state when we moved in and took years of work to turn it into what we wanted. It was a struggle to buy and required two mortgages, but it's ours now and has made us all very happy.

When we still lived in the smaller house, there was no room for me to have a study. Bernadette and I have had a child in all four of the places we've lived, and until our current home, it was always a squeeze. I told her recently that we can never move again — a fifth baby would be too much, too late. She wasn't amused.

I'd had to find and rent a place downtown, in a backstreet building with offices filled with artists and writers. One author lived there full time, which wasn't officially allowed but nobody seemed to mind. I suppose it was very cheap accommodation for him, but there was nowhere to shower and very little comfort. He must have been terribly lonely; I felt sorry for him. I did notice far too many empty Scotch bottles outside his door.

On the ground floor of the building was a store that catered for the BDSM community and made all sorts of leather clothes, equipment, and some things I couldn't quite work out. The owner gave me a guided tour. In the back room were rows of aging southern European ladies gossiping away, working on their machines, and making bondage gear for people's fetishes. While I was being shown around, an assistant shouted to the manager, "It's that woman about the dildos again. Any luck with the brown one?" He answered, "I've told her so many times: we have white dildos and we have black dildos but we don't have brown dildos." Then, as an aside to me, "You see, dildos are a very personal thing."

This was also the time my radio and television career began, and I owe it to Allan Slaight. He was a radio pioneer, a media mogul, and president and CEO of Standard Broadcasting. He was also a fan of the *Frank* diaries as well as my other columns and arranged for me to come to CFRB radio — the most high-profile talk-radio station in Canada — to be auditioned. I appeared on a debate panel, they liked what they heard, and I was offered a weekly spot. After a few months, there was a movement of hosts and I was asked to present the evening show, 7 to 10 p.m.

This was the beginning of a relationship with CFRB, and its later identity as Newstalk 1010, that would last for many years. I'd leave, return, be fired, be rehired, several times. Over the years I'd guest-host afternoon and morning shows, present a lunchtime discussion program, and appear on all sorts of panels. I'm grateful to Allan Slaight, who was very good to me and always a gentleman. His son Gary was my direct boss at CFRB, and while not

Working for 1010, called CFRB back then. I seem to be
interviewing the invisible man.

everybody got on with him, beneath a tough exterior he was generous and forgiving. When Standard sold its stations to a major
corporation, which in turn would sell it to others and eventually
to Bell Media, Gary said to us all, "You'll be sorry I left. You don't
know how good it's been." He was right.

I spent many years at CFRB and also a short period at one of
its smaller rivals, 640. Yet I've mixed feelings about it all. It often
brought out the worst in me, and talk radio is too often built on
the idea of conflict, even anger, when it's not necessary. It's also
conservative by nature, and most attempts at liberal or left-wing
versions of the genre have failed. That doesn't excuse me, because
nobody was forcing me against my will to do the job, and I was

handsomely rewarded. Three hours of radio is long, too long, and to motivate people to call in, I had to use hot-button issues and, if I'm honest, provoke discord. I tried to provide balance and also constitute some intelligent commentary, but the flavour of the show was conservative and harsh. We had lots of guests on the show. They were invariably treated with respect, whatever their opinions, but I was becoming a right-wing radio host.

It was very rare back then for the medium to be able to raise the level of public debate because there's so little time for discussion, and so many of the people who called were regulars who had pre-existing agendas and had already made up their minds. They also wanted to win an argument, push a point, rather than discuss a subject that might be quite complex and nuanced. I often tried to change the style of what we did, but it rarely worked, and we returned to the usual format: black and white, right and wrong, good and bad. Satire and comedy were also frowned upon. I could sometimes be very funny and make a lot of people laugh, but it needed only one or two complaints for management to tell me to stop. Those managers varied, from the supportive and friendly to the distant and severe.

Most of what I said on radio was pretty ordinary and non-controversial, and I didn't always take up a conservative position. I remember hosting an hour-long discussion of the first Iraq War with three members of Toronto's Arab community, where we all condemned the war and argued that it would solve little and probably make matters far worse. I interviewed people who had experienced tragedy and loss, I moderated debates where all sides had their say, and I gave time and a platform to leading left-wing figures. But my show, whatever its time slot, was at heart conservative and often pushily so, and for that there's no one to blame but myself. I'm grateful for the work it gave me, and for the exposure, but it wasn't a happy or rewarding time for me.

I did win a number of awards in Canada and the U.S. for my radio work. The one I'm most proud of is when Toronto experienced the Northeast blackout of August 14, 2003. This was radio as it should be. The blackout was a widespread power outage throughout the Midwest and the northeastern U.S. and much of Ontario and lasted only two hours in some places but up to four days in others. It was then the world's second most widespread blackout in history. I was by chance on the air for much of it, and the only means of communication for most people was a battery-powered radio.

It was a warm evening, air-conditioning units didn't work, lights were off, and people gathered on their front decks or even on the street, used flashlights or lit candles, found out what was going on through radio. The studio was large enough to have a back-up generator so we could be heard. There was a genuine sense of apprehension and even fear out there. Could the police cope with any theft or violence that might occur for such a long period of darkness, would emergency services be available if people were sick, what should people do? Radio came into its own, as though from another age. I was able to reassure people, give them instructions provided to us by the emergency services, play music that would soothe and comedy tracks that might amuse people and relieve the tension. It was one of those truly communal moments usually forced on us by crisis, and it was a privilege to be able to be part of it.

Newstalk 1010 would eventually bring me back as a panellist, but it was in a different format and one I genuinely enjoyed.

It's quite common for private radio broadcasters to be paid to advertise on air. Companies depend on their commercials, and private radio stations depend on companies paying them to run those commercials, the cost being calculated according to the length of the ad and the time and place it airs. The ratings of a particular show are always taken into account. These ads are repeated at various times, and to a large extent it's what keeps private radio on the air. Sometimes hosts are invited to record the ads themselves or even become involved in the campaigns. I recorded ads for a decorating company, a kitchen store, an insurance broker, and, largest of all, a new car rental outfit. The company offered cars for rent and lease at extremely reasonable prices, so much so that the large car manufacturers and sales companies didn't like them at all. In a deeply mysterious move, the bank suddenly pulled the loan that kept the company afloat in their first year, forcing them to close down. The rental company always saw something very sinister behind it all, but I wasn't privy to it. I just recorded the ads and said the owners were good people, which they were, but that didn't stop critics from accusing me of somehow being personally responsible, as though no television or radio personality had ever before promoted a product or company that had failed. Even now, almost thirty years later, someone who takes a dislike to me will say, "He promoted a car company that went bust — you can't trust him." But then people say all sorts of things.

Although I was on radio, I was still writing for a whole parade of publications. *Books in Canada*, *Quill and Quire*, the *Law Times*, and *Snowbirds* magazine, as well as the major newspapers. A new daily newspaper, the *National Post*, had been established by Conrad Black, and although I was never offered a regular column — an insider told me that I was regarded as not always toeing the line, of which I was rather proud — I contributed columns every few weeks. I also completed my Conan Doyle biography. It was adequate, but others have written about him with far more skill and knowledge. I also produced two book collections of essays, and there would be more in the years to come.

I'd also moved from Random House to Stoddart Publishing, a large Canadian house that was having great success with its books and authors. Random House has treated me well, and I'd return there for two more books many years later, but Stoddart was expanding and ambitious. It commissioned me to write a biography of the Christian writer C.S. Lewis, aimed at young readers. The publisher asked for a twenty-five-thousand-word book that could be read by teens or by adults as an introductory biography. This was too tempting an offer to refuse, as Lewis had been a continuing and central influence on my life.

There have been, predictably, numerous attempts to discredit or dismantle the author of the Narnia stories, *Miracles*, *Till We Have Faces*, *The Screwtape Letters*, and so many other books, but it never works. He still speaks so clearly, and so convincingly, especially in an age where condescension toward Christianity is considered a fashion statement. Lewis experienced that in his own lifetime, and in his 1952 book *Mere Christianity*, wrote,

> There is no need to be worried by facetious people who try to make the Christian hope of "Heaven" ridiculous by saying they do not want "to spend eternity playing harps." The answer to such people is that if they cannot understand books written for grown-ups, they should not talk about them. All the scriptural imagery (harps, crowns, gold, etc.) is, of course, a mere symbolical attempt to express the inexpressible.... People who take these symbols literally might as well think that when Christ told us to be like doves, He meant that we were to lay eggs.

Born in Belfast in 1898, he moved from atheism to theism, and eventually to Anglican Christianity in his early thirties. It was an emotional as well as intellectual conversion. "I believe in Christianity as I believe that the sun has risen," he would write after his conversion. "Not only because I see it, but because by it I see everything else." As an Oxford professor, he was highly regarded for his academic writing but disliked by many of his colleagues for his combination of faith, popularity on radio with his Christian broadcasts, and literary success, especially as a children's author. No change there! It's partly why in 1954 he accepted the chair in Mediaeval and Renaissance Literature at Magdalene College, Cambridge. Lewis's friend and secretary in his final year, Walter Hooper, once told me, "He felt as if some of Oxford society was jealous of him, some embarrassed, and some downright hateful."

He did have friends, however, and was a central part of the Inklings, a mostly Christian reading, discussion, and drinking club. J.R.R. Tolkien was one of the members. It was a quintessentially male gathering, and Lewis — and his friends — always assumed he'd remain unmarried. Then came joy: Joy Davidman, in fact, an American, Jewish, divorced ex-communist; about as unlikely a companion as could be conceived. They fell in love, and while the play and especially two films about their relationship, all called *Shadowlands*, may have overly romanticized the story, it was certainly an extraordinary and profoundly touching partnership. They met in 1952 and married four years later, mainly so that Joy could receive a visa so as to continue to live in Britain with her two sons. Whatever the reason, an authentic love developed, and when Joy died in 1960, Lewis was a broken man. He wrote in *A Grief Observed*, still one of the finest books about loss that I've ever read, "No one ever told me that grief felt so like fear. I am not afraid, but the sensation is like being afraid."

He turned down a CBE because he thought it "too political," gave most of his book royalties away to charity, rejected several offers of ordination, and when one of Joy's sons reverted to Judaism, did all he could to help the boy in his faith. In other words, he wasn't a typical evangelist, then or now. But that doesn't fully explain the constant flow of popularity. He had an outstanding intellect, he wrote beautifully, and his grasp of imagery and argument was pristine. But what was so important was that he knew how to write "for" rather than write "down."

Walter Hooper again: "He told me once that he wrote to communicate, and that if ever he forgot that or lost the ability to do so he would simply give up writing. He received so many letters from people who said they had found faith or answers because of what he's said or written, and it delighted him. He never became tired of it. Delighted him."

My book did fairly well but exploded after the first of the Chronicles of Narnia movies came out. *The Lion, the Witch and the Wardrobe* appeared in 2005 and suddenly publishers all over the world were looking for a relatively brief and readable biography of C.S. Lewis. We sold the book to the U.S., U.K., Japan, Greece, Turkey, France, Norway, Poland, the Czech Republic, and Germany.

The Lewis book was followed by a similar volume about J.R.R. Tolkien, a friend of Lewis and author of *The Lord of the Rings* and *The Hobbit*. This was a more difficult book to write because apart from being an author, father, and husband, Tolkien led a relatively quiet life as an Oxford academic. There were only a few stories I could tell, but they were good ones. For instance, in 1938, when far too many people, Christians included, were still ambivalent about Hitler's Germany, a Berlin-based company considered a German translation of *The Hobbit*. Tolkien told his publisher that he deemed Nazi race doctrines to be "wholly pernicious and unscientific." The German publisher eventually wrote to him, asking for a guarantee of his "Aryan descent." In his response, Tolkien dismissed the definition as absurd, and then explained that he was not Jewish: "I regret that I appear to have no ancestors of that gifted people."

Once again, we sold the book to numerous foreign publishers and each time we did so, as the author I received 50 percent of what was paid and Stoddart received the other half. When the movies of

*The Lord of the Rings* came out, sales of the book increased accordingly. I did very well out of these two books and had a third one on the way but was frustrated at how long the royalty payments were taking. I was owed thirty thousand dollars, which today would be worth more than fifty thousand. I was told that it was on the way and there was no need to worry. That didn't help much, and I was disturbed not only by the delay but because the publisher already had its half of the money from my books. Then I woke up one morning to look bleary-eyed at a newspaper and read about a major Canadian publisher going bankrupt. Blimey, I thought, someone is in trouble.

They were, including me. Stoddart had gone bust and there was nothing I could do to get the money it owed me. The Writer's Union went to bat for authors who had been so badly treated, but the best it could get for us was a fraction of what was owed. My wife and I drove to the enormous Stoddart warehouse to buy as much "stock" as we could put in the car. We went back several times, fetching hundreds of copies of my books that were being sold off at a massively reduced price, before they were pulped. I'd eventually sell them all at speeches and lectures, but it took years of hard work and carrying heavy cases of books around the country. The glamorous life of an author is not all that glamorous.

Television came along at around the same time, making the Stoddart loss slightly less painful. My friend Paul Roberts had been asked to host a show on books at TVOntario, to be called *Imprint*. It was under the direction of the new producer of arts at the station, Daniel Richler, son of the novelist Mordecai Richler and himself a former host on a Toronto music show. Paul had all sorts of gifts, but hosting a TV show wasn't one of them. It didn't work at all, and Paul seemed nervous, erratic, and even unprepared. One critic referred to it as "Catastrophe," a pun on the famous, highly regarded French books show *Apostrophe*. It was slightly unfair — but only slightly.

I'd been hired as a researcher on the show, but when Paul was let go as a host, Daniel Richler took over himself and brought on a group of what were called contributing interviewers. There were five of us, including novelists Barbara Gowdy and M.T. Kelly, and dub poet Clifton Joseph. We would be given various authors to interview, and our sessions, fifteen or twenty-five minutes long, would later be incorporated into the show.

One of my most memorable interviews was with Anne Rice, who, sadly, died in 2021. The author of *The Vampire Chronicles*, she'd obviously been asked so many times about the genre that there was not too much else to say. I wanted to discuss her interest in and writing about faith, and this pleased her no end. We went way over time, continued after the cameras were off, and remained in touch long after that meeting in Toronto.

Daniel Richler and I also became close, spending a lot of free time with each other; I think we were bound by a common English upbringing. We played squash two or three times a week and were quite evenly matched. After one game the person who was taking the court after us stopped, looked at us both, and said, "You're the bald one from the radio." In that Daniel had a great deal of hair and wasn't on the radio, I assume he meant me.

The other television show I appeared on was *Studio 2*, also on TVOntario. This was a new program on the province's highly regarded public broadcaster. The format was for me — a white, Christian conservative — to debate Irshad Manji, a Muslim woman of colour. The segment lasted around ten minutes and was called Friendly Fire, a misnomer because we clearly didn't like each other.

Years later, we would become good friends and appear on panels and TV shows together. I always remember meeting Irshad by chance on the street a few years after our show had ended. She said, "Michael, I think we've both done a lot of growing up." She was right, and we hugged. Friendly Fire was, as its title suggests, based on heated exchanges about the news and ideas of the day. I haven't seen it in years, and hardly ever watch or listen to myself, but it did have its moments. It ended after two years and nobody at TVO even called me to let me know.

That's unusual for TVO, where I've otherwise always had a very good experience. Steve Paikin was then the co-host of *Studio 2* and would eventually become the only host of its successor, *The Agenda*. Steve has been a friend for thirty years and is one of the most honest and honourable people I've ever met in media. Actually, one of the most honest and honourable people I've ever met. He's an excellent broadcaster, more informed about his subject than most, and he always allows guests to speak and be the subject of the interview. I do wish interviewers would understand that they're the catalyst, the vehicle, the spark, and that it's not about them. In my next life as a priest, Steve spoke twice at churches I was involved in, and always refused to take a fee. I can't claim to be that generous.

At one time, Steve co-hosted with Mary Hynes, another outstanding journalist who would host the CBC radio weekly documentary show *Tapestry*. It was at this time that I also met and became friends with Evan Solomon, another journalist, broadcaster, and former editor whom I admire so very much. All these people have a humility and humanity that is vital to good character.

Some people have one of those qualities, some of the other, but few both. I'd once been on a London bus with Colin Welland, shortly after he'd won the Oscar in Hollywood and when he was all over the British press. A woman sitting across from us began to speak to him, and the conversation went on for ten minutes. At the end, she got off with a smile as broad as the street we were driving on. "Doesn't take much, does it," Colin said. "She deserves my attention at least as much as one of those movie stars in California." Humility and humanity.

I'd eventually leave *Imprint*, as it changed format and another television opportunity was offered, but it came about at the same time that I experienced ill health for the first time in my life. Obviously, I'd had flu, colds, and stomach aches, but nothing like this. I honestly thought I was dying. I'm far from being a hypochondriac, and hardly ever go to the doctor. I've broken bones and teeth playing rugby, had bad cuts, fevers that probably should have received further attention, but I never bothered. My wife always says I'm extremely brave, but I think it's more laziness than courage. But this was different. I began to feel mild but constant nausea, which is far more enervating and unpleasant than it sounds. Not for a few hours, but almost all the time. I tried every remedy that was suggested but nothing seemed to help. Then I felt occasional sensations down my arms. It wasn't pain, but something I can best describe as a ripple. After this came a slight tightening of the throat. Again, not bad or painful but nevertheless there, and worrying. I had dizzy spells, I couldn't eat, sleep was difficult, and it was all getting worse.

One night it all was so bad that I finally surrendered to those around me and went to the emergency department of the local hospital. They heard the symptoms and assumed a heart attack. It seemed ridiculous that a fit young man with no family history of early heart disease would be having a coronary, but the doctors and nurses were taking no chances. They were excellent, did what they had to in such circumstances, examined me with machines I'd not seen before, took lots of blood, told me at one point, "This is probably going to hurt" (never a good thing when a good doctor says that), and eventually told me that I was in very good shape and I certainly wasn't having a heart attack. Thank God. See, it was nothing.

The "nothing" wouldn't stop. I even went to the trouble of increasing my life insurance, confident that the medics didn't know what they were doing and that I was going to die. I'd never felt anything like it before. I had further tests on my stomach, an MRI, and a scan, and apparently there was nothing wrong with me. Our lovely GP, a man of great experience and wisdom who knows me well, said one day, "Do you think it could be stress?" I was insulted. That's for middle-class moaners; I'm a working-class hero, we don't get stress, the Second World War, soccer violence, work for a living, are you kidding, and similar BS.

My wife was in the waiting room. The doctor called her in to speak to her privately. He then gestured to me to join them.

"Right, Michael. You're doing three or four jobs, often getting just a few hours of sleep a night, sometimes hosting a morning radio show after an evening television gig, writing constantly, travelling all over Canada to give talks, returning on the red-eye so as to work first thing in the morning, and keeping an entire family together on your own efforts. You've had deaths in the family, where you had to sell a lot of your possessions to be able to afford to take the time off and pay for flights, and you never have a day off. And you think stress can't get to you!"

Even then I was reluctant to agree. But he was right. He prescribed Paxil, a trusted SSRI drug, and within two days, it occurred to me that I felt what is best described as normal. Not high, not euphoric, just ordinary. The sensations had gone and have never returned.

Over the years, I've met countless people who take some sort of medication for stress, depression, and anxiety, and it's usually for the best. But these drugs are over-prescribed by overworked doctors. They're not candies, they can have side effects and long-term consequences, and should be given and taken with caution, and only when necessary. When my father died, my mother was already suffering with early dementia. She was given an antidepressant. That was outrageous! She was grieving, which is entirely natural and doesn't require chemical intervention, and she was ill. Perhaps something to help someone sleep at such a time, but only for the short term.

I came off Paxil a year later and did it very gradually. It wasn't easy but I thank God that the medication was there to help me. More than this, the whole episode gave me an understanding of how powerful and influential the brain is regarding our health. The experience started my involvement with mental health campaigns and my determination to help change the way we regard people with mental health challenges, and to increase funding to the area and educate people about the reality of living with mental illness.

One of the saving graces of all this was my wife and family. We have four children, but I don't often write about them, and never post photos on social media any longer, because those who dislike or hate me — usually ultra-conservatives who detest me for my defence of 2SLGBTQI+ people, women's reproductive rights, and a progressive view of Christianity — will use any means they can to try to hurt me. They've targeted my daughters in the past, and I have to be extremely careful to guard their privacy. So, I won't be writing very much about them or about my wife, who has also been included in these attacks. Daniel, I've already mentioned; then we had Lucy, then Oliver, and finally Elizabeth. Some people argue that children push their parents apart, as if there's a couple sitting on a bench and first one, two, then four (in our case) little people come along and sit between them. They do, but it increases the warmth and the bonding; it made Bernadette and me closer. I don't think I can say very much about parenting that hasn't been said elsewhere and doubtless with far more skill, but here's something I wrote when Lucy was grown and about to be married. It applies to all four of our children, who are by far the best thing I've been involved in producing.

When Lucy was a tiny child, just turned four years old, I took her to see *The Nutcracker* in Toronto — that annual event of pristine Christmas escapism. There she was, in her party dress, with a smile and enthusiastic anticipation, sitting on her booster seat and leaning in as if magnetized to the ballet, its music, and its fantasy. Then the music ended, the audience applauded, and we left. At which point she began to cry. The tears bisected her miniature cheeks, and she was nothing but weeping and sorrow, and it was as if my life was collapsing before me. Why, Lucy, why? She had seemed so exquisitely happy. "Because," she said, in between gulps for air, "because it's stopped and it's finished" — more agonizing gulps — "and I don't want the magic to be over. I don't want the magic to end." Now it was my turn to feel tearful. But I managed to reply, "Darling, I promise you, I promise you with all I have, that the magic will never end."

It was an enormous promise to make — the earnest, naive kind parents use that, in the eyes of the child, only burnish their mythical status. But it's also the kind that infers a kind of control that parents eventually come to realize they do not have.

Then the child turns into the teenager, who becomes the young woman, who is now the beautiful, brilliant woman who has lived everywhere from New Zealand to Paris, and Oxford to Canterbury. And now she is getting married.

I will give a speech at her wedding, and there will be no clichés — no *I'm not losing a daughter but gaining a son*, and so on. But I don't know what I will tell her. I want to tell her, in the simplest of terms, that I love her. But that phrase seems weak here. It's a phrase so often used and abused to explain, to sum up, to justify, and even to forgive a whole ocean of emotions and actions. What I feel is more complex than that. After all, the common idea of a parent's love for a child feels superior, protective, even condescending, when really, a parent's relationship with a child is symbiotic. Any mother or father who assumes that they are the exclusive guide and guard of their child should think again. Children make the world appear much more dangerous and vulnerable, but also far more exciting and new again. They teach just as much as we do — and in Lucy's case, I think I've more often been the student.

So instead of "I love you," I will tell her that I've often failed. Not through lack of effort, and often owing to too much rather than too little concern, but that I got it wrong more times than I can count. That contrary to those syrup-soaked greeting cards, genuine love doesn't mean never having to say you're sorry — but saying it almost all of the time.

Instead of "I love you," I will tell her that a father's love for a daughter means knowing when one is wrong, trying to repair damage done, empathizing with what can seem bewildering and even intimidating, letting go instead of holding on, and seeing the autonomous splendour in a child instead of trying to glorify a version of the parent. Parental love is rejoicing in the shock of the new, and singing the metaphorical songs and poetry of a new generation that does not belong to us.

Instead of "I love you," I will tell Lucy: you changed me. My parents are gone now, and how I wish they could have seen their precious grand-daughter be married. But the ages of humanity have to pass, as they always have, and always should. Lucy, I know that I too will not be with you forever, and that hurts me and I know hurts you. I have done what I could and tried my inad-equate best. But please know, my darling, that I am more proud of you than I could ever say, and that what I told you more than two decades ago still holds true. Not because of anything I could ever do, but because as long as you want it to be so, the magic never ends. The music may stop, the dance will finish, and the curtains may draw, but the magic never ends. When I say "I love you" on your wedding day, I will mean all of this.

□

An era, a stage, in my life was coming to an end. Books would take a back seat for a hiatus because television, columns, and public speaking were about to become the driving force in my working life. I was commissioned to write a biography of Mordecai Richler, who had enjoyed my earlier biographies and agreed that I should be allowed to write the book. He said we shouldn't call it an "official" biography or people might think it was hagiographical and soft.

But, he said, he'd tell all his friends that they should speak to me, and he would give me as much time as I needed. "Just don't write about the time I was on the fancy-dress contest at the children's Purim party, when I dressed as Queen Esther," he joked.

Mordecai was an easy man to speak to, and to drink with, and I enjoyed his company. The problem was that to do the job properly, the author had to be soaked in Canadian culture and, even better, in the English and Jewish Quebec culture that Mordecai had grown up in. I wasn't, and I wasn't very interested in it, either. I know that likely sounds condescending, and I apologize, but it's the truth. And unless a subject grips you as an author, a good biography is impossible to write. I tried my best, made several journeys to Montreal, but in the end concluded that no book would be better than a bad one. The publishers were extremely disappointed, but they understood. Naturally, I had to return the advance, and it was substantial. I paid back every penny.

My faith life at the time was fluid, in that it wasn't always at the same level, was often water thin, and I was never sure where it would lead me. The nasties out there sometimes accuse me of changing religions all the time, and I think my Wikipedia entry (I haven't read it in a while, but last time I looked, there were numerous errors) says the same. It's untrue. As I've outlined, I was raised in a home that was culturally Jewish but as my maternal grandmother wasn't Jewish, I'm not either, and was raised without any faith. I became a Christian in the mid-1980s and have remained one ever since. I did walk away from the Catholic Church for a whole variety of reasons, some of them I think entirely understandable, but returned a few years later. Try as I might, I could never stop those Christian waves from splashing at me. I was soon to become a whole lot wetter.

# CHAPTER FIVE

---

# CATHOLIC MAN

In 1998 I was approached by the television evangelist David Mainse and a senior producer who was working for him; they told me about their plans to start a Christian-based television station. It was to be called CTS, the Crossroads Television System, and in order to fulfill the requirements of the Canadian Radio-television and Telecommunications Commission, they needed a certain percentage of what was known as "balanced programming." This had to be non-religious and offer various and different points of views. They asked if I'd be willing to host a nightly current affairs show as part of this required programming. I said I would but assumed this would be the last I'd ever hear of it. Canada, I was sure, would never have a Christian television channel.

To my genuine surprise, the producer called me back a few months later, said they'd received the official go-ahead, and would be starting up the following year. Was I still interested? I was, and *Michael Coren Live*, later *The Michael Coren Show*, would be on the air from early 1999 until June 30, 2011, when I left for the Sun News Network.

For twelve years, almost every weeknight, I would present a show that brought in hundreds of guests, started people's careers, broke stories, and featured interviews with most of Canada's political, cultural, and faith leaders; international authors and thinkers; foreign politicians; and countless people who were making significant contributions to the world. As well as Canadian premiers and prime ministers, this list included Israeli prime minister Benjamin Netanyahu, Sinn Féin president Gerry Adams, Ulster Protestant leader Ian Paisley, and numerous MPs from around the world, as well as filmmakers and award-winning authors, cartoonists whose work had led to international uproar and violence, and even some of the cast of *The Lord of the Rings* movies.

The Gerry Adams interview was interesting for a number of reasons. I'd grown up in Britain with Adams a seemingly ever-present face on the television screen. Irish politics had been constantly in the news since 1969, and Adams was usually at the centre of it. He was president of Sinn Féin between 1983 and 2018 and while repeatedly named as a leading member of the Provisional IRA, had constantly denied it. He's highly intelligent; I could tell that he was reading me as soon as we met. He was also curious about who I was and what I believed, which wasn't always the case with guests, especially if I was only one of a series of interviews. I remember he asked me about my family, and I told him the names of my wife and four children. More than three hours later, shortly before he left, I asked him to sign one of his books. Without ever taking a note or asking me to remind him, he wrote, "To Michael, Bernadette, Daniel, Lucy, Oliver, and Elizabeth."

Ian Paisley was large, loud, and charismatic. He served as leader of the Democratic Unionist Party from 1971 until 2008 and co-founded the Free Presbyterian Church of Ulster. He would be first minister of Northern Ireland from 2007 to 2008, and for many came to represent the face of hard-line fundamentalist Protestantism and loyalism in Ireland. His eventual softening and ability to work with republicans whom he had previously condemned in the strongest language was utterly remarkable. Speaking at the Northern Ireland Assembly, he said, "Today at long last we are starting upon the road — I emphasize starting — which I believe will take us to lasting peace in our province."

I interviewed him twice when the peace treaty was still far off. The first time I met him, the show was still using a phone-in format, and one very Canadian, very polite lady called in and said, "I hope I'm not being rude, and I do apologize if I am, but I heard that you once said, and I am sorry for being so forward, but here goes, and I apologize again. But, well, I heard you said that the Pope was, well, that he was the anti-Christ." Without missing a beat, Paisley roared back, "Well, he is the anti-Christ," and the entire studio seemed to rattle. The caller replied, "Oh, thank you very much," and said goodbye. A culture clash.

The usual composition of the show was three or four guests, all representing different points of view, who would debate and argue fiercely but fairly. I made sure of that, kept order, checked times, and questioned all of them. I presented an opening monologue about the issue of the day, often had a strong opinion during the debate, but never tried to silence an opposing point of view. If I had done so, those guests who disagreed with me wouldn't have continued to return. But they did. We had discussions on the Middle East, religion, sexuality, economics, arts and culture, European politics, and virtually anything and everything else. I also devoted the entire hour to one guest if I thought the subject worthy, which is almost unheard of on North American television. I regard myself as being well informed, always did further research when necessary, and I challenged people, especially politicians, in a manner fairly unusual for Canadian broadcasting. I was never rude but was some-times forceful. I was conservative on many issues, but sometimes went further than that. While I participated in as well as chaired arguments, and always promoted open platforms for most ideas, if not all, I realized later — and perhaps even knew at the time — that I could be fierce and too determined. It's pointless and damaging to give oxygen to an obvious lie, the denial of a historical fact, or a thuggishly hateful agenda, but within the very broad purview of contemporary ideas, I believe most subjects should be given room. If they're wrong, defeat them rather than silence them. I wish that was a more common view in contemporary television.

The studio and facilities at CTS were as good as anything in Canada, which came as a surprise to many of our guests. We had several cameras, a boom operator, a state-of-the art studio, and skilled and experienced directors. There were two researchers — who worked diligently — a producer, and me: a staff of four. That we put out a daily show for so long is, when I look back on it, quite the achievement. We began as a phone-in show but I campaigned to remove the phones and devote all our time to interviews. My view is that while guest callers can occasionally add to the product, it's far more a radio creature, and can even become intrusive. Viewers wanted to see experts rather than listen to their neighbours.

Viewing figures were surprisingly good for a TV show that had very little media coverage, and one that, with a few excep-tions, was available only in Ontario and Alberta. We also made the news quite often. One of my frequent guests was Mohamed Elmasry, an engineering professor born in Cairo who had founded the Canadian Islamic Congress. I enjoyed his contributions and he, in turn, seemed to enjoy being on the show. On October 19, 2004, he appeared on a panel to discuss Israel and Palestine. We were dis-cussing the Palestinian resistance movement and Elmasry said, "Let me give an example — one example from European history. If you look, actually, at the resistance of the French against the Germans, they did the same thing. They blow up bridges. They did kidnap people; they assassinate people ... They assassinated soldiers and their collaborators, and French civilians."

I replied, "But, Mohamed, I think that's a rather tenuous argument. I mean, I know a little about the war and the French Resistance and the lack of it, sadly, but I can't remember one case where the French Resistance, communist or Gaullist or nationalist, would go into a school where German children were and kill them all."

He agreed that children were innocent. I then asked him about women. "The same, if they are women in the army." So, I continued, "Everyone in Israel and anyone and everyone in Israel, irrespective of gender, over the age of eighteen is a valid target?"

He said, "Yes, I would say."

At that point, we went to a commercial break. During that break I told Mohamed that I thought he was being too broad and perhaps would like to clarify when we returned. I said, "I've got to tell you I think you've just dug a very large hole for yourself there. I'm not unsympathetic, and I do believe that Israelis use way too much force and I believe that Palestinians are blanketed with the term 'terrorist,' which is very unfair, but what you've said there, I believe, is very dangerous talk."

But my guest remained firm in his position. This was strong political discussion and what the show was about, so I thought little more of it. Others had a different view.

The next day, Elmasry's remarks were highlighted in the *National Post*, and they then spiralled in to other Canadian newspapers, television, and radio, and then to international media. We were in the centre of a storm that was not of our creating. I was accused by some people of purposely trapping Elmasry, when the opposite was the case. I had offered him a way out, a chance to refine or define his views. I always did this when I thought a guest had misspoken, for the sake of decency and fairness but also for the good of the show. I was fortunate that a number of people in the Arab and Muslim community came to my defence, usually because they'd been on the show themselves and we had a good working relationship, and sometimes a lasting friendship.

But criticism is inevitable, even necessary if you're doing the job properly. I was condemned for having the political scientist Norman Finkelstein on because of his controversial and radical views on the Israel-Palestine conflict. Some members of the Jewish community were outraged. I was criticized for interviewing Kurt Westergaard, the Danish cartoonist whose picture of Muhammad wearing a bomb in a turban led to assassination and attempted murders from Islamic extremists. That time, members of the Muslim community were outraged. If the host of a television show that covers politics and conflict is never in hot water, they're just not doing their job properly.

There were also plenty of apolitical shows, where interesting people would simply tell their stories. One Remembrance Day, we had three veterans of the Second World War on the show. They were wonderfully mischievous and not at all maudlin about what they'd gone through. They were compelling storytellers, too. One spoke of his brother having been killed at the beginning of the war when his plane was shot down during a mission. My guest had wanted to get involved as soon as he was old enough. "I suppose I wanted revenge," he said. He too joined Bomber Command, but after several safe missions, his plane was hit. It was at night, it was dark in the aircraft, and the rest of the crew made their way to a hatch and jumped out. "But I couldn't find a hatch, we were going down, and everything seemed upside down. I knew I was going to die. All I could think of was my poor mother, who would now lose both of her sons. Then, suddenly, there was a crewman standing two or three yards away and beckoning me toward him, and he was standing over the hatch. I thought they'd all bailed out, but obviously not. I looked at him, he looked at me, and then I jumped. It was only after my canopy opened and I was floating down that I realized who that man had been." A pause. "It was my brother."

Was this post-traumatic stress, confusion caused by fear and drama, or perhaps a wishful fantasy? He told me that everybody has some form of prosaic explanation, but he knew what he saw. He was tough, self-mocking, cynical, realistic, and someone who'd spent a long time in a harsh POW camp in Germany. I don't have an explanation, but he had no doubts.

His friend had a very different story. He had been a Canadian tank gunner in Belgium. They were young men, understandably nervous, and had been warned that there were German tanks in the area. Suddenly, they saw the turret of a tank emerge from the side of a house. They were certain it was the enemy and as soon as it edged forward, they fired. They hit the target, but as the smoke cleared, they realized it was a Canadian tank. They counted all of the crew who got out of the tank unhurt, thanked God they hadn't killed anyone, and were then called to immediately move on to engage the real enemy. Fast-forward thirty years and there was a knock on the door of the man's house. It was a new neighbour asking if he could borrow a bottle of gin because they'd run out at the housewarming party they were having. "Of course," he said, "wait here and I'll go and fetch one." When he came back, the visitor said he'd been looking at the man's photographs on the wall, of his time in the war. He saw that he'd been in tanks. So had the visitor. He asked where. Turns out they'd been in the same area. He asked for more specifics. Apparently, they'd been in the same town. The visitor then described in precise detail that his tank had been coming out from behind a house when it was hit and that when the smoke cleared, they realized they'd been hit by one of their own. "The bugger didn't even stop to see if we were okay — just drove off."

My guest paused, took a deep breath, and then said, "Oh my God, I'm so, so sorry. That was me. Don't know what to say. That was me."

I asked what happened next.

"He called me a bastard and then we became firm friends."

I'm often asked about interviews that were particularly memorable. There were so many, and the answer wouldn't be obvious. Most politicians are nervous of saying the wrong thing and celebrities are usually promoting a movie or television show. One that took me a long time to come to terms with was when the father of a murdered child came on to discuss the experience of violent loss. His son had been kidnapped and killed by a notorious pedophile. He seemed incredibly controlled and elegant and had spent years dealing with this obscene tragedy. I, however, couldn't stop thinking of my own sons, young at the time and so powerless and perfect, so eager to smile and laugh, and so dependent on adults for their safety and welfare. I found myself shaking and with tears in my eyes, especially when he recounted how while the killer was driving the boy away, the child said, "That was my home we just passed." In the end, this bereaved man comforted me rather than me him. The murderer had died in prison; I said this must have pleased the father of the poor boy. "No," he said. "I didn't feel anything. I had completely expunged him from my life and my consciousness. It's the only way."

Another interview I'll not forget was with Izzeldin Abuelaish, a Canadian-Palestinian medical doctor and author born in Gaza. He was the first Palestinian doctor to work in an Israeli hospital and was active in promoting Israeli-Palestinian reconciliation. During the Gaza War in 2009, his three daughters and a niece were killed by Israeli tank fire. His moral intelligence and his ability to forgive and to grow made me feel terribly inadequate and meagre.

There was also the transgender woman who came on the show when we devoted the full hour to interviewing four trans people. This was many years before the subject became a major issue in the public square and we received a number of complaints, including from inside CTS. She told me of her relationships with her children from an earlier marriage and how difficult it had all been. There was such an honesty about it all, such a human and loving dimension to an issue that has now become dreadfully polarized and raw. When the human replaces the political, almost anything is possible.

I was allowed to do all this because of David Mainse, the founder of CTS and one of the finer people I've met. He hosted the *100 Huntley Street* television program, was president of Crossroads Christian Communications, and was one of the world's premier television evangelists. He had raised enormous amounts of money for the poor and the needy, both in Canada and abroad; he had transformed Canadian television; and for two generations, he had changed the lives of countless people. He was active when there was an enormous and deserved distrust of televangelists. Several had been revealed to be liars, frauds, and abusers, and those who weren't often spread the most vile and right-wing vitriol. Not that David was liberal, and I disagreed with him then and more so now about some of his views. But he was nothing like his U.S. counterparts, and welcomed into his studio people who would be banned from their equivalents in the U.S.

David died in 2017, aged eighty-one, but his legacy is a grand one, professionally and personally. When my dad had a very serious stroke, I flew out to Britain to see him. It was a very difficult time. I was at my parents' house when the telephone rang early one morning. It was David Mainse, calling from three thousand miles away. "How's your dad? How's your mum? How are you? What can I do — how can I help?"

There was something quintessentially Canadian about David Mainse. While American Christian leaders have often become far too involved in party politics, David was always scrupulous in keeping his party affiliations, if he had them, to himself. He seemed to believe, and bless him for it, that Christians are to be found in every party and that it would be unfair to take sides. David brought me in to CTS, his CTS, and defended me when there were many who wanted me gone. I had labour and socialist leaders on the show, champions of the 2SLGBTQI+ community, Palestinian activists, militant atheists, and all sorts of guests not popular with the usual evangelical Christian audience. CTS should have shown me the door. David would have none of it.

David may have been very protective of and good to me, but I can't say the same for all of those in authority at the station. They moved the show around the schedule, from 6 p.m. to 9 p.m. to 7 p.m. and most spots in between. I was allowed to do largely what I wanted but there was one person who acted so unprofessionally that if I hadn't been reluctant to put my job at risk, I would have complained about him. He once asked me to explain what I was doing when I had a conversation with a colleague in my car, in the car park after the show. When I think back on this, it's outrageous. The person in my car was someone I worked with, a man vital to my show, and we were in fact talking about various guests. But the content of the conversation is irrelevant. "You were seen," I was told. I've no idea what he thought we were discussing, but the sense of paranoia was incredibly disturbing. I did protest but I don't think it made any difference.

This wasn't unusual from this particular man, and while others were less unreasonable, they were often unfair. I once had a sizable wage deduction because I'd used one of the vans we owned, which brought in guests from around the city. My car was being repaired and the vans were already scheduled to make the journey. One more passenger would make little difference. I went to see one of my bosses. I hadn't been told this would happen, I said, the van was on the road anyway, and I'd sometimes driven in guests myself if they were on my route, and had never charged the company. I was told that I was right, this was inappropriate, and that he would "pray about it." It must have been a long prayer because I still haven't been compensated.

I'm extremely grateful for the opportunities that CTS gave me and will always be thankful to David Mainse, but when I made the decision to leave the company, it was one of the better days of my life.

Even then I only left because of their behaviour. CTS had started or planned various projects that I never thought realistic and was now obviously facing some financial challenges. I was asked to meet with the senior producers, who outlined to me what they seemed to think was a tremendously exciting development for my show. They intended to make it an 11 p.m. phone-in program. There would no longer be any guests because no money remained to transport and pay them. In other words, they wanted a late-night radio show on television. It would have been a disaster, would have ruined the legacy and memory of what had often been very good television, and the change was demanded not because of anything I had got wrong. The entire idea was absurd, and I can't believe they weren't aware of that.

At the same time all this was happening, I was receiving repeated telephone calls from Kory Teneycke, who had been trying for months to persuade me to join the new Sun News Network, of which he was vice-president. He offered me more than twice as much money, a generous severance clause, and my own one-hour prime-time show. I'd turned him down in the past and if CTS had been fair to me, I might well have done so again. Not now, though; not with such a slap in the face from one side and such a golden offer from another. When I told my employers at CTS that I was moving on to another position, their reaction was extremely odd. Those I had worked with directly didn't say very much at all, but one of the most senior people at the station virtually told me off. I no longer had to worry about keeping my job, so I told him what I thought, and then asked him what he'd do if CTS had made him such an offer. He seemed genuinely shocked, as though this was the first time he'd heard about it. Perhaps it was. I'd given up caring.

I'll always be proud of some of the things I achieved at CTS. I'd won numerous awards and prizes for my show and had boosted the station's reputation and spread its name internationally. I knew I'd made the correct choice, but the final show was more emotional than I thought it would be. After all, this had been my home for a long time. I recorded the last show and walked with my guests back to the green room. I thought there might be a send-off, a gathering of people who would say cheerio, even a speech and a few tears. There wasn't. I was hurt by that.

Sun News was a radically different environment. My new show was called *The Arena with Michael Coren*. Kory Teneycke was the driving force behind the concept, and while I've taken a different political path from this major player in conservative politics, I like and admire him very much. He was a generous and caring boss and a considerate and giving friend. I remember when my son Oli tore his anterior cruciate ligament playing soccer. "Go, take as much time as you need, and don't worry about money," he said. "This is important, and you need to be with him. You'll be fully paid. Come back when you can." You don't forget those things.

But in television terms, Kory wanted something entirely different from my CTS show. He was looking for a hard-hitting, relentless conservative program that was to be very similar to all other evening shows on Sun. The model seemed to be Fox News in the U.S. Kory was paying me a lot of money and had a perfect right to ask for such a product. I wish it had been otherwise and that I could have given him a tighter, better version of what I'd done for more than a decade, which had been very successful, but that was not to be. Sun wasn't about balance, but about promoting a political point of view. On the other hand, it was an exciting opportunity to try something new and to work for a new media platform that might just succeed.

I joined Sun quite late, after it had initially launched, because I was still at CTS and thought I'd be able to continue. When I did come over, it was to replace another host, and my brief was to reconstitute the show. I was given an excellent producer and a researcher, and all the shows shared a first-class technical, camera, and audio crew. The on-air personalities were a collection of well-known conservatives — me, Charles Adler, Brian Lilley, Ezra Levant — and a set of largely apolitical reporters who were simply doing their job. The producers and researchers were similarly mixed. Some had pronounced conservative politics, while others were looking for a job in television. Charles Adler would leave Sun early and later change some of his opinions, arguing that conservatism had changed so radically that he could no longer identify with the ideology. I was more of a social conservative, having long been a supporter of the welfare state and progressive economic policies.

At first, I enjoyed the show, relished the buzz around the place, and found the novelty of it all personally refreshing and professionally stimulating. But the repetition of right-wing views and the monotony of our output began to drain. I did try to inject some balance when at all possible, but after repeatedly being told by senior staff that this wasn't what they wanted, I gave up. Not something I'm particularly proud of. Sun News was what it was, and I went along with the rest without very much dissent.

When Sun News came off the air, I was relieved for myself but sorry for those who had lost their jobs. I'd been evolving in my views and ideas for some time, and at one point the executive producer called me in to take me gently to task because I was "confusing the viewers" with some of my opinions. It was an absolutely justified criticism, and if Sun had remained on air, I would probably have had to resign before very long. I was beginning to choose to interview people who didn't fit into the Sun News pantheon, such as 2SLGBTQI+ community leaders and progressive Christians. I was also disagreeing on air with people I was expected to support and challenging them on some of what I thought was their rhetoric. On one show, a gun advocate from the U.S., whom I was interviewing in a studio in New York, suddenly ripped off his microphone and walked out. I'd asked him questions he didn't appreciate. On another, a supporter of a right-wing political party in Greece made an official complaint about me when I suggested, quite rightly, that her party was sympathetic to fascism. It was all becoming increasingly uncomfortable.

While I was at the Sun News Network, I also had a weekly syndicated column with the *Sun* newspapers, as I had done for a number of years. All the hosts had a *Sun* newspaper column but mine predated theirs by several years. Yet when the TV station closed down, my column was stopped along with those of most of the other hosts. I was told that the editors were rethinking their approach and I'd hear back from them. Naturally, I never did. After so many years, it would have been courteous for them to tell me I was fired, but whatever their behaviour, it was actually for the best. Neither the Sun News Network nor the *Sun* newspaper chain was my home any longer.

I'm grateful for their long-term employment, and I've always liked and respected the long-time *Sun* editor and columnist Lorrie Goldstein, even though we now disagree on all sorts of issues. Brian Lilley is another person whose views I oppose but have never had a cross word with, and these things matter. We're bound by humanity and should be able to disagree without dislike. But for the paper itself, it may be wrong of me to say it but in all honesty I hardly ever read it even when I wrote for it.

During this time, I'd returned to the church of my baptism so many years earlier, and made my views widely known. Because of this, and because of my relatively high media profile, I was asked to write columns for Catholic newspapers. I wrote every two weeks in Canada's *Catholic Register*, and I also wrote for Britain's *Catholic Herald*, and several other online and printed Catholic publications in North America, Europe, and Australia. I won several awards, including first place in 2013 for best regular column by the Catholic Press Association of the United States and Canada.

McClelland & Stewart in Canada noticed all this and approached me to write a defence of Roman Catholicism, a book they decided to call *Why Catholics Are Right*. It would be on the Canadian bestseller list for eleven weeks and would achieve more sales internationally than I ever thought possible. The book filled a need at a specific time in Catholic history, when many more conservative Catholics were looking for just such a volume that made accessible arguments for what they already believed.

The mainstream media hardly touched the book, and when they did, were mostly negative. Our only foreign sales were Britain and Poland. But the alternative, Catholic media were zealously supportive. Catholic media — television, radio, newspapers, and magazines — are extremely large in the U.S., and I became a regular guest and contributor. *Why Catholics Are Right* was followed up by two books on similar themes. *Heresy: Ten Lies They Spread About Christianity* in 2012, and *The Future of Catholicism* a year later. Both did well but not on the scale of *Why Catholics Are Right*, whose sales were as strong as ever.

I was also being asked to speak all over Canada and the U.S., sometimes once or twice a week. I'll always remember being in Fort Worth, Texas, on a Friday night, and Saskatoon, Saskatchewan, on the Sunday morning. It was December, and I'd gone from +20°C to −25°C in thirty-six hours. I've lost count of how many red-eye flights I took to get home from Alberta, Manitoba, and British Columbia; how many times I changed flights in Dallas, Chicago, and Atlanta. I saw a lot of the American continent, but mostly from hotel room windows and church or meeting-hall doors.

Reading those three books more than a decade later, I can see some of their merits. Of *The Da Vinci Code*, for example, I wrote,

> Dan Brown states that five million women were killed by the Church as witches. In fact, modern research has shown that the witch hunts began in the sixteenth century in Europe and that between thirty thousand and fifty thousand men and women were burned to death for the crime of witchcraft. However, 90 per cent of those trials took place before secular tribunals in countries such as Germany and France, where by the 1500s, the Church had lost most of its influence in judicial matters.

And:

> The Catholic Church built and ran hospitals, schools, and centres for the poor and unemployed generations before the secular state became involved, and even today a visit to almost any main street in the Western world or to a village or town in the developing world will show Catholic charities and outreach organizations operating in what are often the most challenging of conditions.

That was all true, but I was far too selective in dealing with the Catholic Church's abuse scandal, and my defence of Catholic teaching on same-sex relationships, contraception, and abortion now shakes and shames me. I was using far too broad a brush to paint over the cracks and blemishes in Catholic history and the Catholic understanding of the human person. But I can't deny writing what I did, and I take full responsibility for any damage it caused. It didn't seem like that at the time, though. I was offered more columns and more regular radio appearances, and in 2011 was given the Archbishop Exner Award for Catholic Excellence in Public Life, "to recognize outstanding lay achievement in advocacy, education, life issues, and philanthropy" by the Catholic Civil Rights League.

I was constantly asked to defend Catholic teaching, particularly on issues of life and sexuality. What that generally meant was defending a conservative position on same-sex marriage and abortion. McClelland & Stewart even asked me to write an entire book defending traditional marriage and making the case against equal marriage for same-sex couples. Thank God I never wrote it.

People have asked me if I genuinely believed it all. Yes, I did. I'd go to weekly confession, often for things that today I wouldn't even consider sinful. I would never miss Sunday mass and was a regular weekday communicant. I believed it all, but what did I believe? Was it a faith or was it an ideology? I'd codified what is in essence a love relationship between the believer and Jesus into a set of rules and regulations. There was no intent to be cruel, but that's simply not good enough. Sometimes I think I did rejoice in provocation, with little if any empathy for those I might have provoked. There were almost twin solitudes. On the one hand, I thought I was helping people to navigate their way through a complex and difficult world, but on the other I could be thoughtless and rude. I've thought about all this at length, and I wish I could say something more constructive. The best I can offer is that when change came, it was deep and wide, and I paid a significant price. I suppose I believed that if I could hold true to what I saw as unchanging Catholic teachings, even if so much of my experience and intellect had taught me otherwise, I'd be okay and my faith would remain strong. I was convincing myself out of insecurity and even fear but not, I think, malice and disregard. Keep to the road lit by Rome and the Catholic Church's catechism and you won't lose your way.

Added to this was the devil of affirmation — I've seen this at work with lots of people in lots of areas. If enough people say that you're right, praise you, and even revere you, it's very difficult to break away and allow all that adoration to fade. We're autonomous beings but we're also the products of other people's estimation. "Michael Coren is a gift to the church," said New York Archbishop Timothy Dolan, in front of a crowded building full of supporters. Who was I to disagree? It delighted me, it inflated me, it seduced me. To reject all that and to rebuild is not just difficult, it's incredibly painful and frightening.

But ropes to the shore of humanity and kindness were pulling on me more and more. My parents had recently died, and it had forced me to think harder about the life I was leading and the life, if there was one, to come. Neither Mum nor Dad had what you'd call "good deaths." Mum was smashed by her dementia, and when she was in the filthy thing's final stages, I'd sit by her bed and silently ask how this could be allowed to happen. This good, kind woman was now a shell of what she had been, unable to speak her pain and her fear, oblivious to the love and care around her. Where was God; why was such horror happening to one so undeserving? Such a question has been asked for all time, and at this very moment is being uttered in agonized choruses as the innocent succumb and their families mourn.

In time, I'd work out a response to all this — not an especially good one, but the best I could do. In theology this problem of God and the existence of human suffering is known as "theodicy" and there are entire books written about it. But in all honesty, it's just a way to intellectualize what is an entirely justifiable scream of sorrow and anger. The letter of James in the Bible tells us to be patient and confident in our suffering, and the great C.S. Lewis wrote of pain being God's "megaphone to rouse a deaf world." But does it explain the death of a child or the horror of a parent? As for those ghouls who insist that pain is a punishment for our sins, that's twisting God into a personal vigilante and is, ironically, profoundly anti-God — even blasphemous. It's also directly contrary to what Jesus said about the sick. He spent an extraordinary amount of time with people who were ill and disabled and totally rejected any idea that their plight was a result of their or their family's actions. But it still doesn't answer the question of why all this happens, and it's in no way inappropriate to wonder at a God who is supposed to be all powerful, all good, and all knowing. A mature faith allows for questions as well as answers, even encourages them, and if anybody wants a complete and satisfying answer, I simply cannot give one. I'd also recommend being extremely dubious about any person of faith who claims otherwise.

My response, for what it's worth, is that our world is merely the land of shadows, and that real life hasn't begun yet. As a Christian, I'm promised not a good life but a perfect eternity. I have hope because I know that Jesus suffered, too, and the Resurrection was the template for all of humanity. I realize this might be inadequate for the non-Christian, but let me also emphasize that I'm convinced the gentle rabbi, the prince of peace, came not only for his followers but for all of us. There's more. He was also us. Was us, and is us. The Christian belief is that Jesus was fully God but also fully human and knew our pain and terror not as a divine onlooker but as part of the human community. This was the unique, the unprecedented miracle of divine empathy. The heavenly leap of God into our lives and our deaths. He wept and He loved, for us and with us. The world in which Jesus lived was soaked in bloody injustice, oppression, and often-gruesome death, and surely it's no accident that this was the time chosen for God to break into humanity. That gives me enormous solace, even when all around me is brokenness and chaos. I worry about my family and friends, I try to comfort those close to me who have lost loved ones, but sometimes I too feel the clawing darkness.

My mum eventually fell into a coma-like sleep, and the dementia took her while she was alone in a distant hospital ward. I wouldn't insult you by claiming that it was all somehow tolerable because of my faith. Mum wasn't a Christian, Mum suffered, and I was angry and I was crushed. I can't pretend that I have all or even any of the answers, but what I've written gets me through the day and gives me hope.

Dad was gone by the time that Mum started to deteriorate. I'm not sure she was even fully aware that her husband had died. I was glad she wasn't suffering, but it broke my heart that we couldn't fully mourn together.

It was the second stroke that took him, but after the first one, something extraordinary happened.

Let me introduce you to my niece Katie, who is what many people would still describe as "handicapped." She was born several months premature and spent a long time in hospital. Katie had two strokes herself when she was tiny and is now classified as being autistic. Which means many things to many people. I'll offer one example.

In a large hospital in England, my dad lies in bed after his first major stroke. There's occasionally some movement, but no speech whatsoever. We all sit around and do the usual hospital things, not knowing what to do or say. Then Katie walks in. No inhibitions;

none of our silly preconceptions and prejudices. She climbs onto the bed, gets under the blanket, puts her arms around her grandpa, cuddles up to him, and falls asleep. She does that because that's what she does when she visits Grandpa at home. Why would a big building with new and strange noises, new and strange smells, and new and strange people make any difference?

And for the very first time in forty-eight hours since he was hit by fate's cruelty, my father shows emotion. He cries, first gradually, and then loudly and openly. Then he moves his head, looks at me, and says my name. We press the call button, and a very young doctor runs in. He looks at my father, looks at the charts, and says, "Wow, this wasn't supposed to happen. You've had a little miracle."

We had. A little miracle named Katie. Dad would have an astounding if not complete recovery.

Katie achieved that because that is what Katies do; what people who are physically and mentally challenged do every day: they cut through the nonsense and the fear and are on the front line of the battle for civilization, teaching those of us who are without disability what honesty and simplicity are all about.

Katie can do jigsaws like Supergirl. She starts not from the outside but from the middle. The complex shapes that so baffle us take form in her exquisite mind. Wonderful pictures come alive and speak — speak in a way Katie cannot. Hey, not *like* Supergirl. She *is* Supergirl. She doesn't have an extensive vocabulary, but then again, sometimes words aren't so important.

When I arrived in England from Canada on one trip, she walked straight up to me, grabbed my hand, and took me to a chair, showing me total and unconditional love. It was as though I'd never left the country — but I had emigrated before Katie was born.

I sat down and chatted to my sister. Had it been difficult? "Yes, but also joyous beyond belief. A new adventure every day and a new path of discovery. Wouldn't change it for the world. Katie has made us all grow so much, taught us things we didn't know about ourselves, about what it really means to be human." At which point Katie trotted her way into our conversation, into our world. She wanted to watch the DVD of *The Jungle Book*. She'd seen it hundreds of times, but that didn't matter. Katie doesn't need expensive toys or fashionable luxuries. She's so much more than that. Perhaps so much more than us.

I increasingly believe that people with disabilities are God's gift to us, to act as a conduit to provoke love in hearts that are sometimes hard and cold. Fly, Supergirl; fly, Katie — fly, you who are mocked and marginalized, as high as you want, and never care about those who would clip your wings, from Britain all the way to Canada.

Katie, my parents' deaths, my children growing up, and my having to face the sometimes rather ugly realities of the media world all led me to start to rethink who I was and what I believed. I was halfway there, had embraced Christianity but was intent on championing doctrines that I was coming to realize had a tenuous link to what C.S. Lewis described as "mere Christianity," or perhaps pure Christianity. I stand by a great deal that I wrote in *Why Catholics Are Right*, but far from all. It was as though I could see the truth through a foggy window but hadn't bothered to scrub it clean and look at what was really there. I was in a warm and comfortable halfway house, and one that I certainly didn't want to leave. I had become complacent, and complacency is never a friend of faith. It was rapidly unravelling, I was changing my views on so many subjects, and each time I did, it forced me to question other aspects of my philosophy — to look hard into how I behaved and what I thought was just and unjust.

In 2014, in one of my final syndicated *Sun* columns, a short while before I was let go, I wrote an article that would open up the floodgates of support as well as of vitriol and change my life forever.

The headline was "I Was Wrong." It was only a first step and now seems very tame and passive, as though I were pulling punches and feeling my way, but my goodness it had an effect.

I wrote:

> I haven't been asked to march in any parades at Pride this year and, frankly, I doubt that's ever likely to happen!
>
> I'm still regarded by many in the gay community as an enemy and I understand that reaction. I have said and written things in the past that, while never intentionally hateful, caused offence and pain. This isn't necessarily relevant, in that truth cannot change according to response, but I could and would not say such things any longer. I was wrong.
>
> In the past six months I have been parachuted into clouds of new realization and empathy regarding gay issues, largely and ironically because of the angry and hateful responses of some people to my defence of persecuted gay men and women in Africa and Russia. I saw an aspect of the anti-gay movement that shocked me. This wasn't reasonable opposition but a tainted monomania with no understanding of humanity and an obsession with sex rather than love.
>
> I'm used to threats and abuse, and as someone who has just completed a book about Islam's treatment of Christians and has campaigned for years for beleaguered Christians in the Muslim world, I am immune to verbal attacks and even death threats.
>
> But this was different. I was accused of betraying my faith. Thing is, I have evolved my

position on this issue not in spite of but precisely because of my Catholicism. My belief in God,
Christ, the Eucharist, and Christian moral teaching are stronger than ever. Goodness, I am even
trying to forgive those "Christians" who are trying
to have my speeches cancelled and have devoted
pages on their websites and blogs to my apparent
disgrace.

The other attack is to argue that I have surrendered to pressure or that my children have influenced me. This is so absurd to be genuinely funny.
My kids? They're not political, they respect and love
me and they would never waste their time trying
to change my mind. That they're accepting of gay
people and gay marriage is axiomatic — they're
aged 16, 20, 24, and 25 — and, whether you like it
or not, that generation in the West simply does not
comprehend opposition on these issues.

As for pressure, you clearly don't know me. I
have never compromised because of intimidation,
even when it comes from genuinely violent and
serious people. It's tragic but indicative that there
are critics who cannot come to terms with growth
and change and, rather than consider what I have
to say, try to question my motives.

No, I have evolved on this subject because I
can no longer hide behind comfortable banalities,
have realized that love triumphs judgment, and
know that the conversation between Christians
and gays has to transform — just as, to a large
extent, the conversation between conservatives
and gays has.

I am not prepared to throw around ugly terms like "sin" and "disordered" as if they were clumsy cudgels, or marginalize people and groups who often lead more moral lives than I do. I am sick and tired of defining the word of God by a single and not even particularly important subject.

If we live, we grow. The alternative is, of course, death.

The column and my final few shows for the Sun News Network provoked a reaction that I'd never imagined. And by the way, I would indeed be asked to march in a number of Pride parades, and I did so with a smile on my face.

# CHAPTER SIX

---

# NEW AND BETTER THINGS

My column in the *Sun* newspaper group produced a response that I wasn't prepared for. It seemed so mild and so personal I assumed it would be one of those pieces that would go largely unnoticed. I've written a plethora of columns for all sorts of newspapers over the years and while you never quite know what the response will be, I was confident that this one wouldn't provoke much of a reaction. How wrong I was. In the end there were more than a thousand emails, letters (some containing bodily waste), death threats, attacks on my family, and calls for my wife to leave me. There were accusations that I was a child abuser and an adulterer, a thief, and a fraud, and that my change of heart was all for the money.

The latter was particularly odd, in that my professional career would largely evaporate in the coming months. I'd lose five regular newspaper columns, fourteen speech opportunities, a book contract, two radio shows, and a television hosting position. There is none so angry as a homophobe scorned. The angry letters ranged

from illiterate screaming to more considered hatred. This was one of
the coherent ones: "Sir, you are probably a homo yourself and you
will be paid with eternal hell and damnation. I see that you are also
a Jew and that does not surprise me. In the pay of George Soros,
are we? Or is it the Mossad and their freemason friends? Yes, yes,
I know, I know." He signed it with "God's peace and love to you."
Well, as least he called me "sir."

A conservative Roman Catholic blog, Contra|Diction!, gave me
perhaps my best headline ever, with *Michael Coren Complicit in
Destruction of Souls Who Practice Homosexuality, Pt 1.* I'm still waiting for the sequel.

The leader of a Catholic group to which I had spoken on more
than a dozen occasions wrote to me in far calmer tones.

> As your friend and brother in Christ, I am con-
> tacting you out of love to discuss a concern that
> has arisen. This is not easy, but Scripture calls me
> to contact you to discuss this sensitive topic. It
> has come to my attention that many Catholics
> are concerned with the video we saw of your pro-
> gram regarding the homosexual charity story. We
> are not sure what your beliefs are on the issues of
> homosexuality, and gay "marriage," as it relates to
> Catholic/Jesus's teaching? Can you please clarify?
> You have always been such a clear, bold voice for
> Catholic truth through your books and speeches
> for some time, but many in the Church are now
> concerned with these recent statements. It's hard
> for many of us to tell if you were affirming the
> gay lifestyle. We are hoping you were merely try-
> ing to emphasize that all people — whether living
> in sin or not — should have a desire to help the

orphaned, poor, hungry, etc. Given how articulate you are, we don't understand the ambiguity on this important moral area. Michael, as your brother in Christ, will you please reply to clarify your beliefs on this issue? God bless you and your family. You remain in my prayers, and please pray for me and my family, as well.

What he didn't say in his letter was that in my speeches to his organization's various branches across North America, from New Orleans to Rhode Island and Indiana to Nebraska, I generally didn't discuss sexuality or gay themes at all, and never, ever made it a key issue.

A few years earlier, I'd received a papal knighthood, and one of the Canadian organizers of the Equestrian Order of the Holy Sepulchre of Jerusalem sent me an angry letter demanding that I resign and return "what we gave you." All they had given me was a small medal and a necklet. I lost the necklet long ago but have to admit I do still have the little medal. Perhaps he thought they'd given me a horse as well.

Even more bizarre was the man who told me that he'd written to "the government" demanding that I lose the Queen's Diamond Jubilee Medal that had been awarded to me in 2012 for services to journalism. What this had to do with anything is still beyond me. I still have, and sometimes even wear, the medal.

I received a much more conciliatory note from Cardinal Collins, then the archbishop of Toronto. He's a quiet and decent man. We had met for breakfast several times in the past two years. It was always at my request; he'd never asked me to meet him. Why would or should he — he's a very busy man — and so this email was extremely unusual. It transpired that he had received an inquiry, a complaint, concerning my stance on the issue of homosexuality. We met for breakfast and the cardinal was his usual gentle self. Mostly we spoke about Catholic education, but then he explained that he had been "sent a video from your nightly television show, *The Agenda*" — I reminded him that my show was actually called *The Arena* — and that he was uncomfortable with it. We chatted, and while he didn't seem to listen very much to what I said, he did tell me that he was concerned with the terms "gay and gay community," and preferred to speak of "people with same-sex attractions," but appreciated that I had to "speak quickly on television."

I tried to explain that I had been struggling with the central mercy of the Gospel message for some time and how I could apply this to loving same-sex couples, but it didn't seem to be moving the conversation forward in any way. This exchange seemed entirely pointless, and I had a feeling that both of us had already made up our minds. What surprised me was that a complaint or two about this particular issue should have caused him to initiate a meeting for the first time. I have not heard from the cardinal since that breakfast.

The host and producer of *Catholic Answers*, a highly influential media platform in the U.S., wrote to me thus:

> Okay, deep breath. There's no soft way to say this, and it wasn't my decision. Hear me out because I'm writing as a true admirer of yours, and — I trust it's mutual — a friend. There is enough consternation and head-scratching among the senior staff at *Catholic Answers* over your apparent change of heart on the matter of homosexuality that we're going to wait before having you back on. Your books as well, for now, are no longer sold on our website. I'm just confused. In the first column, the reason you give for your change of heart (new realization and empathy) is the reaction you

got from some people to your defence of human rights for persecuted homosexuals in Russia and Africa. You also never really say what you were wrong about, exactly. That you regret using words like "sin" and "disordered"? It made me wonder if you would endorse using them if they didn't sound like clumsy cudgels. A reasonably intelligent reader could conclude that you don't believe same-sex attractions are objectively disordered ...

And so on and so on.

After Sun News went dark, I'd been asked by the Christian television show *100 Huntley Street* to appear as a guest host. I'd conducted a number of interviews about faith and science, the Armenian genocide, ISIS, education, and various other issues. I never spoke about homosexuality because I knew the views of those who produced and hosted the show and respected our differences. They clearly enjoyed my work; they called me "the intellectual" and booked me to record more interviews for them. I'd spoken to the producers at *100 Huntley* about my position on the gay issue, telling them I wouldn't discuss the topic on air, and we agreed that there were so many other subjects to discuss. They were satisfied and told me I was "far more of an asset than a liability." Then just a few days before I was to record my next interviews, I received an email from the executive producer: "I trust this email finds you well. This is a difficult conversation that I need to have with you. With the high public profile you have in media and social networking in relation to gay marriage and the Catholic Church, it is felt that we have to part our ways as an organization."

I replied that we had already discussed this and that I'd agreed not to refer to the subject on air. His reply was "people know what you think."

By now the letters telling me that I was fired were becoming monotonous. Some were curt and dismissive, while others took time to explain why my services were no longer required. Lawyer friends said that in some of the cases, I had grounds to bring a lawsuit, but that approach has never appealed to me.

On top of the evaporation of work was the abuse and the libel. It kept coming, sometimes it hurt, but after a while it became like background noise — I didn't really notice it.

More considerate people asked me why I had changed, and that was an entirely reasonable question. I suppose that a number of things had happened with an eerie coincidence of timing. In 2013, Uganda's biting homophobia smashed into me. Canada's then foreign minister, John Baird, gently criticized a Kampala official about proposed legislation to further criminalize homosexuality and even to make it a capital offence. Baird, who had been a great defender of persecuted Christians, was stridently condemned for criticizing "noble Uganda" and questioning its independence. I was outraged at Uganda and aghast at the treatment of Baird, and I said so on television and in print. I honestly thought that conservative Christians and the 2SLGBTQI+ community could come together on this issue, put aside differences — albeit briefly — and work to try to stop Uganda attacking people simply for being who they were. This had nothing to do with marriage, I argued, but was about simple humanity. How naive I was. My pleas were not only rejected, but I was accused of "selling out" and being on the wrong side of the argument.

It was close to the demise of the Sun News Network. For one of my last shows, I invited on one of the women who had criticized me. Surely, I said, you can't support the idea of Uganda executing people for being gay. Her reply chilled me. Execution would, she said, "be unwise." Unwise!

Shortly after this, World Vision in the U.S. announced publicly that it would employ Christians living in same-sex relationships.

There seemed to be no pressure for World Vision to change its previously strict code of sexual ethics, which had declared that no employees could indulge in sex outside of marriage and that marriage was between one man and one woman, but still they did so — because, I assume, some people at World Vision obviously realized that there were gay Christians in committed relationships who wanted to help the poor, the starving, the broken, and the sick. Within moments of this entirely innocuous announcement, however, the evangelical and wider Christian world went into retaliatory overdrive. Leading pastor and author Rick Warren; Billy Graham's son, Franklin; and the leaders of entire denominations suggested that donation money would disappear unless World Vision changed its mind, and some went so far as to advise their congregants to withhold financial support. It was a virtual boycott. World Vision's behaviour was, these Christians claimed, totally unacceptable; there was talk of the evil one, of dark forces, and of hell. Then, lo and behold, World Vision announced it had reversed its position, and it was very sorry, and it wouldn't happen again.

In less than two days, it had fundamentally changed its theological beliefs over a point of profound moral understanding and ethical teaching. It was a humiliating and embarrassing affair, and all sorts of people should have been deeply ashamed of themselves. Yet many of those very people seemed proud rather than sorry. What I couldn't understand was what the marital status or the sexuality of someone had to do with their heartfelt desire to help starving African children or Indian families living on the streets. Can gay people in committed, life-long relationships not clean wounds, not hold the dying, not empathize with the desperate? Perhaps, it could be argued, they can do so more successfully than someone who has not been marginalized by mainstream society and by certain churches. Can a gay person in a committed, life-long partnership not raise money for the starving and work tirelessly for the poorest of the poor? It seemed obvious to me they had been doing so for decades, and for generations, and have often done it rather well. Their sexuality was irrelevant to the people they were helping and mattered only, and a great deal, to some of those who claimed to share their love of God.

I felt as if I were being pushed against a wall of uncertainty, and that what I'd long regarded as secure was being dismantled daily. My defence of traditional Christian teachings on the gay issue was, I'd always assumed, based on love rather than hate, but now I started to question myself. Was it all a self-defence mechanism, a comforting denial of truth? I decided to reach out to Vicky Beeching, whom I'd seen interviewed on British television about her sexuality and Christian faith and who was described in the *Guardian* as "arguably the most influential Christian of her generation." She would probably disagree with that opinion, but given her many appearances on television and radio, as well as her substantial following on social media, hers had become a powerful voice for change. Beeching had been an extremely popular singer, musician, and recording artist on the North American Christian music scene, but the main reason for her new prominence was that she'd announced to the world, and to the evangelical Christian world in particular, that was she gay. Hiding her sexuality for many years had caused Beeching to develop severe health problems, and she was still struggling with the demons of intolerance, hatred, and enforced secrecy. Within the world of North American Christian music, homosexuality is considered profoundly sinful, and when she came out, her career was promptly destroyed. To this day, she is still routinely attacked in the most severe and hurtful ways.

She was eager to help me. We chatted at length and eventually met in person in London. I found her to be utterly inspiring. There was pain but no malice, no anger. She'd written a book about her experience, *Undivided: Coming Out, Becoming Whole, and Living Free from Shame*, and I'd recommend it to anyone who has any interest in this subject.

Beeching told me that when she came out, she'd "hoped deep down that they might react differently."

> I knew the majority of evangelical Christians around the globe believed that same-sex relationships are sinful, shameful, and wrong. But because my songs were sung in congregations around the world every Sunday, and because I was loved and respected by that entire community, I'd wondered if they might react in a slightly more open-minded way. But they didn't. It was immensely painful. Almost all the evangelicals I'd known and worked with told me I was "choosing sin" and stepping away from God in my decision to come out. They also told me I was no longer welcome to sing, or speak, or continue in any of the leadership roles I'd held at evangelical conferences and events. It was extremely damaging to my mental health to feel so excluded from my former community, as they'd felt like family to me since childhood.

What so moved me was her quiet determination. She said she had no regrets about coming out, had found it healing and liberating, but that it had come at a great cost. "I lost my career in Christian music, my livelihood and financial security, and my sense of belonging within the evangelical world. But overall, it was absolutely worth it. The fear I battled every day was so intense and the toll it was taking was too great — I had to step into the freedom of being the person I was meant to be."

There was also such a generous optimism in Vicky, such a compelling confidence and determination:

> The global church changed its mind when it formerly opposed William Wilberforce and the ending of slavery. The church also changed its mind when it previously opposed the suffragettes and the right of women to vote. Eventually, we'll see that same equality and social justice extended to people who are LGBTQ — and I'll do all I can to play my small part in moving the church toward that goal. I hope I can help change minds and hearts and bring greater awareness. LGBTQ equality is not something the church can ignore. I hope books like mine can help spark the conversation and change minds and hearts.

I decided to dive into Scripture again and look at what it said on the issue, to explore without prejudice and without wanting to draw conclusions that would support my Catholic view. What I discovered was extraordinary. The Bible can be as gentle as a watercolour and as powerful as a thunderstorm. It can be taken literally or taken seriously but not always both. It's a library written over centuries, containing poetry and metaphor as well as history and biography, and without discernment, it makes little sense. It has to be, must be, read through the prism of empathy and the human condition. The thing is, the Bible hardly mentions homosexuality, which is of course a word not coined until the late nineteenth century. The so-called "gotcha" verses from the Old Testament are specific to ancient customs and are often misunderstood. The Sodom story, for example, wasn't interpreted as referring to homosexuality until the eleventh century. Lot, the hero of the text, offers his virgin daughters to the mob in place of his guests, so it can't exactly be used as a compelling morality tale.

Ezekiel in the Hebrew Scriptures says, "This was the guilt of your sister Sodom: she and her daughters had pride, excess of food, and prosperous ease, but did not aid the poor and needy. They were haughty, and did abominable things before me" (Ezekiel 16:49–50). The Old Testament never speaks of lesbianism, and its mentions of sex are more about procreation and the preservation of the tribe than personal morality and romance. It also has some rather disturbing things to say about slavery in Genesis and in Paul's Letter to the Ephesians, about ethnic cleansing in Deuteronomy, and even killing children in First Samuel. So, a precise guide to modern manners it's certainly not. As Christians, we need to read and understand the Hebrew Scriptures through the prism of the New Testament, and to grapple with the reality of what they are: a history of an ancient people, containing shining morality but also troubling events and laws, culminating in the life, death, and teachings of Jesus Christ.

Jesus doesn't mention the issue, and St. Paul's comments, mainly in his letters to the Romans, are more about men using young male prostitutes in pagan initiation rites than about loving, consenting same-sex relationships.

There is, however, one possible discussion in the New Testament. It's when Jesus is approached by a centurion whose beloved male servant is dying. Will Jesus cure him? Of course, and Jesus then praises the Roman for his faith. The Greek word used to describe the relationship between the Roman and his "beloved" servant indicates something far deeper than mere platonic affection.

Then there's the love of David and Jonathan, Jesus refusing to judge, and the pristine beauty of grace and justice that informs the Gospels. Most of all, there's the permanent revolution of love that Jesus didn't request but demanded. His central teaching, remember, is to love God and love our neighbours as ourselves. We're told this in three of the four Gospels — Matthew (22:35–40), Mark (12:28–34), and Luke (10:27). It's a transformational moment for Christians, to know that only by loving others can we properly know and love God.

After this I met with gay Christian groups, who were disarmingly kind and generous and shamed me with their gratitude for my small steps away from what I had previously preached and written. I read the works of people to whom I shall be ever grateful, who had walked this road long before me. The scriptures that I assumed had underpinned homophobic Christian views seemed to blow away like dust in the Judaean Desert, but that wind sometimes stung me, and so it should. Because genuine faith is like sandpaper of the soul, rubbing away at the being of faith. It hurts, it draws blood, but in the final analysis it should lead to a more perfect believer. I suppose that the Divine Carpenter had begun work on me, because I went through what I suppose was something like a spiritual breakdown. I cried, I couldn't sleep, I questioned everything I'd done. I'd always believed in God, always embraced the Christian message, but now it seemed to me that I'd got it all so terribly wrong. I was no fool, I knew Biblical languages, I read voraciously, I had life experience, but it was as if I'd walked through my life with some sort of comforting theological myopia.

I devoured more books that were suggested on the subject and myself came across one called *Fathomless Riches: Or How I Went from Pop to Pulpit*, by the priest, author, broadcaster, and former pop star Richard Coles. I'm fortunate enough to have got to know Richard a little, and whenever I've mentioned how influential he has been on my life, he's modestly dismissive. But it's true. The memoir of this man, whose gay sexuality and profound faith were not only entirely compatible but beautifully symbiotic, touched me deeply. Richard says he's never had any problem with reconciling his faith and his sexuality and that being gay is just "a variation on the universal theory of human sexuality." Yes, yes, yes!

□

The abuse continued and became worse the more outspoken I was. I became largely immune to it, but what did disappoint me was the refusal on the part of my Christian critics to acknowledge that people can change — isn't that, surely, what the Christian message is all about? We can be, have to be, born again. Instead of listening to what I was saying and considering why I had retained my faith but changed some of the beliefs that came as a consequence of that faith, the critics attributed false and base motives to me, or just threw insults. They tried to silence me, too, and I soon discovered that cancel culture is alive and well on the right. It wasn't just that I lost so many jobs, but whenever someone tried to hire me, they came under a barrage of pressure to reverse their decision.

In May 2015, for example, the *Prairie Messenger* asked me to write a column for them. I asked if they knew what had happened in my life, and they said, courageously, that it was precisely why they wanted me in their newspaper. I told them what the consequences might be, but they insisted. My first column was about a ten-year-old Paraguayan girl. I wrote of "a terrified little girl victimized by those around her and forced by a government to give birth to the child of her rapist. That is not justice, that is not life, that is not right. God must be weeping." They let me go a few days later, but unlike most of the others, it was with regret and genuine sorrow. The campaign to have me fired had simply been too strong.

I should have been shaken by all these dismissals, but in a curious, trusting way, I was always sure that it would somehow all be okay. None of this was about money or income, anyway, and whatever the outcome, I had no choice. I couldn't live a lie. Not because

I'm especially noble, but because I think that doing so would have killed me. I was also feeling happier and healthier than I had for years, despite the things that were being said. I felt a little like Ebenezer Scrooge on Christmas morning. It wasn't too late, I had been shown the world's possibilities, I could start again and afresh, make amends, try to put things right, follow Jesus Christ absolutely and not partially. Love triumphs over law, the words of the Son of God over those of the sons of Pharisees, and we shed a skin of fear and misunderstanding to put on the cloak of understanding and community.

In 2014, I had lunch in downtown Toronto with the publisher of a leading gay internet site. We talked shop, laughed, and drank wine. Family came up, and I showed him some photographs of my wife; he remarked on her good looks. There was a long pause. He turned his phone around and showed me a picture of his husband. Then he looked up: "I was hesitant to show that to you. I was uncomfortable with how you might react."

I felt ashamed and very small.

"You know," he continued, "you had quite an effect on my life. I'd just come to Toronto, wasn't even out yet, and I was meeting with a colleague. He went off to the washroom, and I read the newspaper he had with him. It was the *Toronto Sun* and you had a column in it that was critical of gay people. Of me, really. It broke my heart."

The two of us are friends now, but that doesn't excuse me.

In 2015, I was asked to preach at the Metropolitan Community Church of Toronto. The MCC is not exclusively gay but its central theme — its charisma, if you like — is outreach to 2SLGBTQI+ people, and in all of its many international branches, it is at the heart of the struggle for full equality. Its leader in Toronto at the time was Brent Hawkes, who was one of the most high-profile, visible, and eloquent leaders of the gay community. It was Brent who personally invited me to speak at the church — we had known each other for years because we often appeared on opposing sides on television and radio. Neither of us ever thought we'd be embracing, close to tears, in front of the altar of his church. I'd spoken to hundreds of groups for more than a decade and hadn't felt nervous for a long time, but I was most definitely nervous this time. How many of these people had I hurt; how many had lives made more difficult by my writing and broadcasting? I'd never hated but I had given an intellectual veneer to the anti-gay movement; had enabled, even unintentionally, some muddy bigotry.

There were two services, with a combined congregation of around seven hundred people. And as I walked into the church on that hot, rainy morning, I sensed no condemnation, no cynicism, no grudges. As an emotionally constipated Englishman, I was several times close to weeping as I witnessed a sense of authentic Christian community that, with all due respect, I have not always found in mainstream church settings. I saw collectives of warmth and support; groups of people from various ethnicities, backgrounds, sexualities, and experiences united in acceptance. After so many months of abuse, accusations, and firings, my sense of liberation was overwhelming. I told them that as a straight man who had reversed his position on gay rights and equal marriage, I had experienced a glimpse of a shadow of a whiff of what it must be like to be a gay Christian. I said that some of the finest Christians I had ever met were people who were gay and had remained true to Jesus Christ. I said that remaining Christian in the face of hostility and even vitriol was an indication of an enormous depth of faith, a living, fleshy example of a glorious mystery. I spoke of unconditional love, of what Scripture actually said about sexuality rather than the popular and misguided caricature of Biblical truth that is so often offered. I said that the only absolutes were grace and love. Never has a standing ovation felt so true, so good, and so pure.

Apologies don't expunge crime, sin, or wrongdoing, but they do acknowledge harm caused and hurt done, and that matters to victims. A genuine act of apology involves full admission of guilt, sorrow for the crime or failing, and fitting compensation, or even punishment. Words of sorrow are not supposed to be some sort of get-out-of-jail-free card, even literally so in some cases, and if that is their purpose, they make matters worse and not better. I've spent years apologizing to the 2SLGBTQI+ community for my outspoken opposition to equal marriage and full equality. As I say, I may never have hated, but I did enable hatred, and could be flippant, dismissive, and carelessly cruel. My very public reversal of view cost me much of my career and income, so I suppose I've paid a price. I've also tried to put matters right with my writing and speaking and have experienced a great deal of abuse because of it. That's a good and not a bad thing because penance is not only necessary in itself, but a prerequisite for absolution. The forgiveness I've experienced has been immensely liberating, and profoundly moving, but there are always those who refuse to accept change and define their credibility by cynicism. Let's be candid here: modern society has often made a fetish out of pain, and those who have suffered the least are often the last to forgive. Be that as it may, the human condition is imperfect. We get things wrong, and the act of apology makes us, and those around us, better and bigger. A forced apology can change a few minds, a rehearsed apology perhaps some more, but a genuine and visceral apology can change the world.

I can't properly explain any of this without speaking about prayer, which might seem irrelevant to some people, but to a Christian, to any person of faith — to me — it's as necessary as food and water. We live in a time when prayer has often been stripped of that nourishment, its substance filtered down until the act seems largely meaningless and banal, rather like a handshake or a casual

"How are you?" It's even used as an emotional weapon: ostentatious Christians on social media explaining that they will "pray for you," the subtext being that you're so wrong you're almost certainly damned. Along with politicians, we have scores of movie actors and sports stars who regularly tell us they are praying for peace, happiness, good weather, and even a win against a rival. Then there are the onlookers at murder scenes, especially when a child is involved. They hold up posters announcing that they are praying, and always seem to find a television reporter who will nod sympathetically as they tell the world they are praying for the angel now in Heaven and praying that the swine who committed the crime will suffer for eternity.

Prayer is mutable, fluid, and various. The first, most central, reality is that it's far more about changing oneself than about pressuring God into action. Because of its intimate nature, we're at our most honest in prayer, assuming in a great thrust of trust that we can say and admit anything. While we do make requests, we more often confess to what we really are, who we really are. That's an incredibly difficult and challenging exercise, and something rarely attempted in modern, secular society. The catharsis, if genuine, is powerful. It's of course inevitable that we also ask for things; that's part of what it means to be human, and beating ourselves up for it is self-defeating. But to reduce prayer to an empty response to a difficult and even terrifying situation, or to a supernatural shopping list, is to misunderstand the act itself.

Prayer is about letting go, allowing, accepting. In a way, it's a profound acquiescence and a sometimes reluctant acceptance that we may not know what is best and that there is someone above and beyond us. But prayer isn't a mere act of self-reflection or even meditation, because that doesn't require a relationship with God. Prayer is a conduit, a bridge, between the Almighty and us. Yet neither is it totally rational, and no believer should try to argue otherwise. Only someone who misunderstands the nature of faith, God, spirituality, and prayer could argue that they're rational.

Søren Kierkegaard put it this way: "Just as in earthly life lovers long for the moment when they are able to breathe forth their love for each other, to let their souls blend in a soft whisper, so the mystic longs for the moment when in prayer he can, as it were, creep into God."

Creeping into God. That goes some way toward explaining what happened to me. I was allowed to creep into God through a new understanding of love. For me, prayer was and still is my anchor of hope when the world seems a very bleak place. I can rest in God, speak to him, listen to him even in silence, and feel refreshed. It's a conversation with the divine that gives my life meaning, purpose, and a place to be refreshed and nourished. Also, I suppose, a place of safety. Not somewhere to hide but, yes, to be safe. I pray all the time but in a formal sense, I now begin each morning in the same chair in the same room surrounded by the same pictures and crucifixes, go through the "Morning Prayer," part of the daily office contained in the Anglican prayer book, and then sit in silence so as to listen. I could no longer not do this than I could not eat or drink.

□

The more I prayed, the more I realized I wasn't comfortable within the Roman Catholic Church and found it confining. My Christian faith was deeper than ever, and the reason I'd changed my view on sexuality was that I'd grown into a deeper relationship with God. There was no way I could walk away from organized religion — I had to have a place to worship, to be part of communal devotion — but the Roman Catholic Church, for all its many attractions, no longer felt like home. I'd been to evangelical churches many times and while there was much to admire there, the theology was just as conservative as, if not more than, the Roman Catholic version, and there was also something emotionally and spiritually lacking in the services I'd attended.

I'd always rejected Anglicanism because I was raised in a vaguely Church of England culture as a child in my first school, and in a country where there is a formal if not always noticeable link between church and state. I had always admired it but didn't take it all that seriously. Yet the people I'd been reading and meeting — such as Richard Coles; the excellent Mark Oakley, who was then at St. Paul's Cathedral in London and is now dean of Southwark Cathedral; Alan Wilson, bishop of Buckingham; Jeffrey John, then dean of St. Albans; and so many others — were all Anglican. If that wasn't God giving me a punch in the head, then what was it?

In the last weeks at the Sun News Network, I'd gone along to the nearby Anglican Cathedral Church of St. James in Toronto for the midday service, partly to escape the right-wing hysteria of some of those around me. I didn't receive communion because Roman Catholics aren't supposed to take communion outside of a Catholic church and, as I've said, I always took the teachings very seriously. These services had only a few congregants in attendance. They were elegant and moving, and very similar to what I'd experienced in Catholic churches — the added appeal of what I saw was a greater humanity and intimacy.

At the last one I attended, I came forward when the offer of the Eucharist was made, received the host, sat back in my chair, and thought, "Now you've done it — now you've really bloody done it." Many people reading this will wonder what the fuss was all about. In fact, they're right — what is all the fuss about? All should be welcome at the table and supper of Jesus Christ, which is something I emphasize now when I celebrate the Eucharist. For me, back then, it did matter — it was more than a symbol, it was a conscious decision to say that I'd moved on.

The separation had been coming for some time and I was too frightened to admit it. I regarded myself as a Catholic and still do, but a liberal Catholic within the Anglican communion. I live my Christianity in a Catholic sense but beyond the confines of papal supremacy and authority because I can no longer accept it. Nor can I accept Rome's teachings on contraception, women's ordination, and marriage. It was rather like a ball of theological wool unravelling. As soon as it began, it was difficult to stop it. It wasn't lack of belief that drove me from Rome, but the very opposite. Partly out of respect for the Catholic Church, I could no longer receive its sacraments and call myself a Roman Catholic while simultaneously rejecting so many of its values and views. I know many Catholics remain in their church while doubting or even denying, but that wasn't for me. I wasn't strong enough.

When the Sun News Network closed down and I wasn't working in downtown Toronto, I began to attend my local Anglican church, St. Martin-in-the-Fields in west Toronto. It's a gorgeous, serious church and its Anglo-Catholic spirituality and services delighted me. Here was everything I'd wanted in Roman Catholicism but without the intrusive politics and the anachronistic moralism: pure worship in a beautiful and serious context. I realized that within Anglican Catholic orthodoxy, I could pursue socially liberal ideas in a church of mingling theologies. I could reach out in Christ's beauty to all people, irrespective of sexuality or religion, and love everything about them. I'd never been happier or felt more motivated as a Christian.

A word or two about Anglican Catholicism. The Anglican Church is broad, containing evangelical as well as Catholic parishes and worship. The latter would celebrate tradition, aesthetics, and music, and holds to the Catholic heritage of Anglicanism. The Church of England may have rejected Rome and the papacy in the sixteenth century, but it remained and remains the church founded by the Catholic pioneers so many years earlier.

On my first Sunday at St. Martin's, I sat at the back of the church, almost hiding, because I had a certain public recognition and didn't want to be noticed. I've no idea why I thought that mattered, but I suppose I was still testing the waters. At the end of the service, a woman in a clerical collar approached me and very delicately said, "It's Michael, isn't it? I know you've been going through a hard time, what with the television station closing down and with your new ideas and beliefs. Are you okay?"

It was a small gesture, but to me it was the size of a new world. I'd had hardly any personal warmth or care from the Catholic priests I'd known, and here was an Anglican priest — and a woman priest at that — showing me humanity and affection. Her name was Susan Bell, we became friends, and eventually she became my bishop, who would ordain me as a deacon and then as a priest. God, as they say, does indeed move in wildly mysterious ways. It was one of the most significant and formational meetings of my life.

A year later I was officially received into the Anglican Church, which is not essential but suggested. It was at the cathedral in Toronto where I had first attended midday services, and there was a photographer outside. He took a photograph of me with Susan. Because I was known, and with absolutely no negative purpose in mind, my photo was then made public. Those who had already attacked me for liberalizing my stance on various social issues now had another stick with which to beat me, and the hate campaign began again. This time I was prepared, but there's always something we're surprised by.

There was a part-time journalist I'd helped when his career was in bad shape. His wife once told a mutual friend, "Michael is the only person who went to bat for him and tried to find him work." He attacked me quite brutally.

A fairly well-known Catholic priest wrote two columns attacking me, leading me to wonder if I really mattered that much.

Because I'd tried to keep my spiritual journey private and personal, I was accused of being duplicitous. I'd spoken to some Catholic groups while on that journey and kept my remarks to the truth of Jesus and the veracity of the Gospels. I never said a word against Roman Catholicism or contradicted Catholic teaching. I was a Christian speaking to other Christians about Christianity. This, my critics said, was subterfuge and dishonesty. It proved my point about an ideology.

There was the usual dose of anti-Semitism and libel. My Catholic wife received two letters telling her that she had to leave me, and I was told repeatedly, even by a Catholic priest, that I was damned. Damned if I did, damned if I didn't. One comment I will always treasure was from the website *Vatican Catholic*. It screamed, "Yes, he's an abomination." I've always loved that one. It's like a tabloid headline about a celebrity giving birth. "Yes, it's a boy."

On top of all this, and more of a problem, was that I had very little media work left. I tried not to worry, but the bills had to be paid. Book royalties from *Why Catholics Are Right* understandably dried up. It had still been selling thousands a year and no doubt would have continued to do so. Nobody would buy it now, and I fully understand why not. I had some contact from people who said they'd be burning it. Not a problem, I'd always reply, because burned or not, I still received a payment. There were a few small and loyal publications that continued to publish me, but nothing close to what I needed.

Then I received an email from Andrew Phillips, the then comment page editor of the liberal, centre-left *Toronto Star*. I'd written plenty of book reviews for the *Star*, but that had been some years ago and I was surely anathema to this grand liberal newspaper. Andrew was sense and sensibility. He'd been fascinated by my story, couldn't guarantee anything long term, had to see how readers would react to Michael Coren being in the paper, but asked me to write a fairly long article on what had happened to me and the reasons behind it. I did, and it went down well. While I started slowly and gradually with the *Star*, I'm now a regular columnist and regard them as my first and main outlet for my writing. They're a joy to work for and I'll be forever grateful to Andrew, to Scott Colby, and to the others on the opinion pages of what is in effect the progressive conscience of Canada.

In time I'd be a semi-regular columnist for the *Globe and Mail*, the TVOntario blog, and the *Walrus*, as well as the *New Statesman*, the *Oldie*, the *Telegraph*, and the *ipaper* in the U.K., and for CNN in the U.S. Outlets come and go, especially in the digital age. I wrote for the CBC, but they stopped taking opinion pieces; I wrote for *Maclean's*, but they've dramatically changed their content; for *iPolitics*, but they lost their freelance budget; for Toronto's *NOW* magazine, but they closed down. I did have a regular column for the *United Church Observer*, but they suddenly terminated my employment. I was actually rather pleased because it wasn't at all a comfortable venue. They've now changed their name, but I haven't seen the magazine in a long time. The national Anglican newspaper did ask me to write one column, which won a national church press award. They said they'd get back to me to write more. That was almost a decade ago, but I'm sure they're terribly busy.

It's much harder to make a living as a freelance or even staff journalist today than it was when my career began. I often hear from young people starting out in media, wanting my advice. I try my best to be encouraging but what I really want to say is, "Have you considered accountancy?"

McClelland & Stewart also came to my rescue. Doug Pepper was an old friend who had commissioned several of my earlier works. We discussed a book partly on what had happened to me, but mainly outlining the Christian case for equal marriage. I know he had a tough time selling it to the other editors at the publishing house, not out of hostility to me but because they wondered if there was a sufficiently large audience.

They had a point. The book was cathartic and, I like to think, important, but sales were disappointing. What it did do was establish me as a Christian media voice on pressing issues, speaking from the opposite side of the arguments from former years. That persona took me years to grow accustomed to. I was increasingly a media voice representing progressive Christian values. I had never expected and never asked for it, but it was becoming vocational, as though I was the right person at the right time — someone who could publicly express and defend what Christ and his followers believed and taught. It also helped me to clarify where I stood and to intellectualize what had often been instinctive. I'd come to believe that Christianity is a romance, and like any affair, it cannot be properly quantified. We might find someone attractive or even exciting, but those qualities are far from unique. It's something else, something beyond the formulaic that leads us to commitment. For me, true love came relatively late.

As my faith has deepened, I have tried to broaden the circle of inclusive love rather than guard the borders of what I once thought was Christian truth. Instead of holding the door firm, I wanted to push it wide open. I'd come to realize that Christianity is a permanent revolution, a state of being in which believers must challenge our preconceptions every moment of every day. The Christian belief is that the death of Jesus on the cross was the ultimate proof of love. It's supposed to be a reciprocal relationship, a heavenly symbiosis and, as such, requires specific actions on the part of the believer. Forgiveness, self-criticism, and contrition; radical action to blanket the world with fairness; standing with those who need that love the most and seldom receive it. It's not easy, and it wasn't supposed to be. It's about a second chance, a lifeline thrown to humanity. It's not about judgment but forgiveness; not about rejection but inclusion. The Jesus story is revolutionary in its most intimate sense because it dreams of peace, equality, and transformation.

I'd found that the loudest voices are often the most raucous, because they are convinced they possess exclusive and infallible truth. It's supernatural certainty that leads to intolerance when faith should actually be a dialogue. For me, it felt downright disrespectful to interpret the Bible as a literal guide to daily living, or even as the inerrant word of God. It's much greater than that — much more profound. It's poetry, history, and metaphor, as well as the revelation of God's will and plan. It's anything but facile, and anything but a dry text to be referred to like some manual for the aspiring moralist.

The Gospel, I now know, is about a first-century Palestinian Jew who grabbed the world and made it new. He demanded that we love God and love others as ourselves, and that we treat people the way we would want them to treat us. That's the faith in all its terrifying simplicity. The rest, as it were, is mere commentary. Yet that commentary has often dominated the Christian narrative in public life. Loud and cruel obsessions with sexuality and reproduction, a support for the powerful rather than the powerless, an identification with Caesar rather than the rebel Jesus.

What I'd come to realize, and should have known earlier, is that Christianity shouldn't be, but far too often has become, a sort of moral thermometer, or a checklist where we can tick off certain boxes and feel good, or bad, about ourselves. It's all so much deeper and grander than that. I was confident in all this but sometimes I wanted to retreat, to turn down the world's volume. Or, to put it another way, to get closer to the filters of God's absolute love. British playwright Tom Stoppard, not known for being a Christian or for defending God or faith, wrote in his usual pithy and delightful way, "Atheism is a crutch for those who cannot bear the reality of God."

With great insight, the strongly Christian novelist and children's author George Macdonald wrote in the nineteenth century, "How often we look upon God as our last and feeblest resource! We go to Him because we have nowhere else to go. And then we learn that the storms of life have driven us, not upon the rocks, but into the desired haven."

I wanted my own crutch, or something resembling a desired haven. I could take most of the abuse, but there was an emotional denting that was far greater than any professional loss. The latter could be partly replaced, but the harm to the psyche cut deeper.

It was then that a friend suggested I train for the priesthood. I thought he'd said "police" and looked at him as if he were mad. "I'm fifty-seven, for God's sake! And I could never have been a cop."

No, he said — the priesthood.

Not for me, I replied, not by a long way. "I'm not cut out for it, couldn't tolerate years of seminary at my age, and my wife, my children, and my friends would think I'd lost my mind."

But he kept on asking, and he wasn't alone.

# CHAPTER SEVEN

---

# AND NOW IT BEGINS

My friend wasn't the only person to suggest the priesthood. Some priests I knew said the same thing, and before long I thought there was some sort of conspiracy. I had lots of doubts and didn't know if I had the energy to spend what would be several years at university, taking courses while simultaneously working in churches, hospitals, and care homes, then another year or so as a deacon. Then there was the chance that even after all that, I'd still be turned down. I didn't know if I had the calling or the ability and skill to do a job that was part public speaker, part social worker, part spiritual counsellor, part office manager, and part celebrant of the most profound ceremonies possible. Could I listen enough, could I care enough, could I do enough, and could I be enough?

Michael Ramsey, former archbishop of Canterbury and a wise and saintly man, said in his book, *The Christian Priest Today*, "You put yourself with God, empty perhaps, but hungry and thirsty for him; and if in sincerity you cannot say that you want God you can perhaps tell him that you want to want him; and if you cannot say even that perhaps you can say that you want to want to want him!"

I did want to want.

What finally convinced me was the argument of someone who was certainly not a Christian. "Doesn't bother me either way," he said. "But if you're going to do it, you need to do it soon. If you give up or fail, big deal. If you don't try, you might have a lot of regrets in a few years."

The words struck home. It would be extremely tough, of course it would, but I wasn't as busy with journalism as I used to be, and I could study at the University of Toronto, just a short subway trip away.

Practicalities weren't the issue, though. I had to consider my relationship with God, which if authentic is at its heart a dialogue, and one that involves questions, arguments, and even doubt. We're made — and if we're Christians, we believe we're made by God — to be thinking individuals who want answers, and not robotic creatures who simply obey. A mature belief in Scripture necessitates an understanding that the Bible is not divine dictation but an inspired history of God's relationship with humanity, which is a wonderful guide to life but doesn't solve every modern problem and hourly challenge. It can be complex, it's often nuanced — some would argue, although I disagree, that it's even contradictory — but at heart it's about absolute love. Christ says not a word about, for example, abortion, homosexuality, euthanasia, pornography, or the so-called traditional family, but demands justice, forgiveness, equality, care for the poor and for the marginalized and for strangers, and compassion even for enemies; he insists on peace and on the abandonment of materialism; and he constantly speaks of the blistering risks of wealth and prestige.

He turns the world upside down, he questions the comfortable and the complacent, sides with the outcast and the prisoner, and has no regard for earthly power and worldly ambition. Love and hope. Christianity isn't safe and was never supposed to be. Christianity is dangerous. Yet, truth be told, we have often transformed a faith that should revel in saying yes into a religion that cries no. Its founder died so that we would change the world, but many of his followers fight to defend the establishment; they try to link Jesus to nationalism and military force, and dismiss those who campaign for social change as being radical and even godless.

Change can be frightening to all of us, and certainly was for me, yet the Son of God told us that fear and anxiety were unfounded. If we worry about the evolving world, we're just not listening to the words of Christ that we claim to revere. It's as though the cosmetics of the Gospels, the veneer of the message, have become more important than its core and its central meaning. Jesus spoke less about the end times than the time to end injustice; less about whom we should love than about how we should love everyone. If we miss that, we're missing the whole thing. The great C.S. Lewis, one of the finest communicators of the faith in modern times and someone I've mentioned several times in this book, once wrote, "Christianity, if false, is of no importance, and if true, of infinite importance. The only thing it cannot be is moderately important."

I decided to reject moderate importance and enrolled at Wycliffe College at the University of Toronto. It's a first-class place of learning that has its origins in the evangelical wing of Anglicanism. It's a thriving and vibrant community of young Christians who come from all over the world to study and learn. My theology was less evangelical and more progressive, but I was confident of receiving an excellent Christian formation and education.

After I'd put my name down and chosen most of my classes, I began to have doubts again. In the end I gave myself another year to reflect and pray about it all. That's a grand way of saying that I needed to give it more thought. Was it really for me; could I embark on something that would be entirely life-changing? It was the right choice, and in that year, I travelled, read, spoke to people who could help me in my decision, and went on prayer retreats. When the time came to enrol again, I realized that I had to make the jump.

My only reservation was in a section of what was called Wycliffe's Statement of Moral Vision. It had disturbed me when I first saw it and it did again. It said, "We are called to follow the norms of sexual behaviour taught by Scripture as interpreted by the universal Christian tradition from the earliest church to our evangelical founders." It wasn't a directly personal issue for me as a straight, married man, and it was open to interpretation. But I thought then, and still think now, that it concerns homosexuality, the rights of 2SLGBTQI+ people, and equal marriage.

I spoke to church friends, some of whom had attended Wycliffe, and they said it really didn't matter and I should just disregard it. They had, they said, and lots of others did, too. There were, they rightly said, teachers and students at the college who dissented, and even those who embraced the code were usually moderate, intelligent, and generous Christians. I was told this wasn't some hard-line school like some of those south of the border. I knew that, but as convincing as this was, I couldn't sign on. It felt as if I'd be betraying all that I'd become, and all the people I'd met in the preceding few years.

In the end I opted to take six of my thirty required credits at Wycliffe College, and I relished my time there. But for my own college, I needed a place where I wasn't required to subscribe to such a statement and where I could feel free to believe and say whatever I liked. I applied to Trinity College, directly across the road from Wycliffe. I was accepted and jumped in. I say "jumped in" deliberately because in the following three years, there would be times when I was convinced I was drowning.

□

Studying divinity at Trinity wasn't exactly what I'd expected. The college is impressive, and Trinity itself is modelled on an Oxford or Cambridge college. It was founded in 1851 by Bishop John Strachan, who envisioned it as an essentially Anglican school. Trinity became part of the University of Toronto in 1904, and over the years the Anglican connection was gradually reduced. But it's still there, and the exquisite, enormous chapel — more a large church or small cathedral, really — proves it. When visitors see the college dining room, they generally think of the hall in the Harry Potter movies (which is actually Christ Church, Oxford). There's a fine tradition of scholarship and learning, and some of the brightest undergraduates in the country go to Trinity.

Divinity students were generally older than the undergrads and certainly more eccentric, but not always in the best traditions of eccentricity. My first encounter with the second- and third-year students wasn't reassuring. Three of them were arguing quite nastily and entirely pointlessly about an obscure college issue; one was manically knitting and taking no notice of anybody around her; and most just ignored the newcomers, as if we were an unwelcome intrusion. Some of them had been at Trinity for quite a long time, and I'm still not sure if they all graduated. At least one potential student, a deeply impressive young woman, simply dropped out of the course when she saw whom she'd be studying with, and I fully understood her decision. I'm delighted to say that she later returned to Trinity and is now ordained. It wasn't that these were bad people — although in one case, there did seem to be genuine malice involved — but that they were so very odd. They'd give us what I'm sure they were convinced was accurate and helpful advice, which turned out to be completely wrong and misleading, and warned us from taking classes with certain teachers, who were actually very good.

Over the next three years, there would be tears, bitter disputes about things that were of no real importance, and a disappointing lack of collegiality and Christian solidarity. It became apparent that the more serious and devoted students had distanced themselves from the rest — from those who obsessed about intricate points of high Catholic worship but didn't turn up for services or came to morning prayer halfway through. There was a large and comfortable divinity common room, and I was told early on, by one of the better students, "Don't spent too much time there. It's fatal."

Yet at the same time, Trinity was very good to me. It paid my tuition, and over the next three years gave me numerous prizes, some of which came with generous financial gifts. The teachers were encouraging, knew their academic fields well, and could at times be inspiring. Of the thirty credits required, some had to be theological, some philosophical, some historical, some practical. The latter included work in churches and in pastoral situations such as hospitals or prisons.

I was fortunate to train and work in two churches, St. Luke's in Burlington and St. Jude's in Oakville. St. Luke's was with Stuart Pike, and he taught me so much about what it means to be a priest. He still does, because I'd eventually go to work with him at St. Luke's, and I hope to be there for many years to come.

The priest in charge at St. Jude's was Rob Fead, and although my course required me to spend three months with him, I ended up being there for a full year. We became friends as well as colleagues, and in his official evaluation of me in 2017, he wrote of "liturgical presence" and "noble simplicity" and said that I "carried out liturgical responsibilities such as serving at the altar, preparing the altar table, reading from the lectionary, distributing communion and praying for the sick with grace and dignity, was prayerful and understood the sacred responsibility, which is not always easy to maintain by the third service on a Sunday morning!" He praised my preaching and my approachability and wrote that I was "open to the God of surprises but also open minded enough to allow his belief system to grow. Michael is not a man with a stagnant faith! He continues to grow in theological understanding and is not afraid to express in the public forum what he believes and Who he believes in."

I was overjoyed, not only because it was such a positive report but because Rob was someone I deeply respected. I thought I might work with him if I was ordained, and we discussed how that could happen. Then, in the summer of the following year, my friend and mentor Rob Fead was killed. He had been riding his motorbike when a truck smashed mercilessly into him, and he died instantly. This good, fine, strong man in the prime of his life was suddenly ripped from his wife and mother, and all those who knew and loved him. The mourning was tangible, and thick with sorrow and agony. Beyond those who knew him closely were those who were helped and made complete by him. Originally a Roman Catholic clergyman, he had later become an Anglican, and was admired beyond words at St. Jude's in Oakville and the entire diocese of Niagara. Part of my grief was that while I'd certainly thanked him, I'm not sure I ever made him aware of the monumental debt of gratitude I owed this invincibly humble man of God.

That, of course, is so often the way. We leave things terribly late and are too clumsy and lazy to tell our loved ones how much they mean to us. Rob would probably have been embarrassed by all of that and told me it was nothing. It wasn't, and in some ways, it was everything. In these days of understandable cynicism about organized religion, and suspicion toward the clergy, the work and achievements of Rob Fead should be painted large and bold. He was, if you like, the real thing. He didn't so much live *by* the Gospel as lived *in* the Gospel, always whispering its compassion, truth, and reassurance.

He was an army chaplain, too, and in 2014 presided over the funeral of Corporal Nathan Cirillo, the reservist who was killed while standing guard at the National War Memorial in Ottawa. "My job, in the midst of all that chaos and fear, was to bring some sense of hope," he said. Hope was precisely what he did bring to all those who knew him. We sometimes visited hospitals together, spending time with people close to the end of their lives, often in lonely discomfort and sometimes in physical pain. As the darkness hovered, Rob managed to show them the light. He held them close, and this robust and tough fellow became to them the spirit of gentleness.

Those who knew him, many of them Christians, naturally looked for explanations and answers about his death. What I said to people back then was that nothing will expunge the grief and the emptiness, that he was taken far too early, but that he had left the world a different place from what it had been before him. He had made it just a little better, splashed it with joy and empathy, and reminded us that we're here to care rather than to judge, and to help rather than to hurt. I still speak to and sometimes see his widow. In a gesture I'll never forget, she gave me many of Rob's clerical clothes, which I still wear when I stand behind the altar and celebrate the Eucharist. I carry some of Rob with me all the time.

His death shook me. I considered taking some time off, but there were still courses to take and work to do and I'm sure Rob would have wanted me to continue to, as he used to say, "get on with it." I did, and enjoyed most of it.

I found that Church history came naturally to me, and I was reasonably good at it, although philosophy and theology were more challenging. I also started to make some friends, particularly among students of my own age but also with some of the younger ones. Being in my late fifties and having some life experience certainly helped in a lot of what we were asked to do. I'd been a journalist for years, and a professional broadcaster, so writing essays and delivering homilies came much easier to me than for some on the course. I might not be as clever or energetic as others, but I could write an essay, knew all about deadlines, and found public speaking a pleasure instead of a terror.

My pastoral work in churches, care homes, and hospitals was more of a challenge. Let's call it a learning experience. Dealing with people who are in pain and distress is an education that no classroom could ever come close to providing. Issues that we read about or see on television suddenly become immediate and living. Homelessness, loneliness, poverty, abuse all have a name and a face.

I remember when Jenny (not her real name) called me because my personal number had been listed as one of the emergency contacts for the church in which I was working. She was hesitant, clearly nervous, and reluctant to be specific. Could we meet? Yes, of course. Two hours later, we were in a Starbucks. It was largely empty at 11 a.m., so we had privacy.

Her story gradually unfolded. She was from the Bible belt area of Niagara, her background was Dutch, and her parents were Calvinist Christians. She had begun running away from home when she was twelve years old because her father beat her, and her mother refused to intervene. "I think she hated it, but she was under his control. I heard her crying sometimes," she said, ignoring her coffee and staring past me, as if she was hesitant to make direct eye contact. The pattern of fleeing and returning continued until she was sixteen, when the violence became intolerable.

I asked whether she'd ever considered calling the police.

"I suppose I should have. But there were cops in our church, in our community, it was all so enclosed. And I was frightened of being blamed. I don't know ..." and her voice trailed off.

She found minimum-wage work in Hamilton. One night, after drinking too much, she went home to the apartment of a young man she worked with. "I know, I know, I know," she said, obviously frustrated with herself as much as with the situation. "He didn't force himself on me but," she paused, clearly embarrassed, "it was the first time I'd had sex."

I muttered some words that were supposed to be supportive, and she understandably ignored them.

"I'm pregnant. I can't go home. I'd have to stop work. I live in a tiny place. I don't know how to look after myself, let alone a kid. As for adoption, that's a crock. It's not easy — there's legal stuff, and I just can't do it. I can't do it!" And she cried.

I referred her to a wonderful nurse who could help this isolated, abused young woman — little more than a girl, really — to enable her to decide to have a termination if she wanted.

Becky came to the church to meet me. She was born in the United Kingdom and had come to Toronto as a child. In fact, her mum and my dad were raised in the same part of London as I was. She had two children, one of them with a disability, and their father had fled the scene as soon as Becky told him she was pregnant again. "No loss," she said. "He was a bastard, and he hit me." She put on a brave face, but I could see she was terrified. Anybody who dismisses the state as being pointless or a waste of money should know that Becky and countless like her can survive only because of social support and housing benefits. Even so, they're limited, and she had to live in very challenging conditions. "I just can't have another child. I know I should never have gotten pregnant again but, well, you know, things happen. The last birth almost bloody killed me. I've got nothing, nowhere, and my body is fucking broken!" She cried, and the bravado was blown away by the dark reality of it all. "Help me. Where do I go? What do I do?"

There was other heartbreak. A woman who had just left a care home where she'd visited her husband, whose dementia had so fogged his mind that he no longer recognized his first and only love. Eventually, he thought his wife was his long-deceased mother.

But that was okay, she said. Just being in the same room as him was enough. As she walked home, a car stopped, and a woman passenger asked for directions. They were gladly given. "Thank you," said the woman, "and please take this as a gift." At which point, she rather forcibly hung a thin necklace around the lady's neck. Only when she got home did she realize that the woman in the car had removed her original necklace and replaced it with a cheap trinket. The stolen necklace had been a gift from her husband.

I went to the police, who were sympathetic and understanding but said there had been a string of these thefts in the last few weeks, and they hadn't managed to catch anyone. "They've probably moved to another town now," the police officer said.

Or the care home where one lady held a baby doll very tight, and another shook her head in constant disapproval. The group didn't respond much to me but did seem to listen a little to the hymns I played on an old CD machine. Traditional and tested prayers, I was discovering, have resonance. I recited them, thanked everybody, and left. At the door, one of the women, who hadn't opened her eyes the entire time, said, "Thank you. You've made my day. My husband was a priest. I loved him very much." Then she closed her eyes again. "That's the first thing she's said in a week," a nurse told me.

Another woman I met with had two small children and was living in an emergency shelter, which wasn't right for all sorts of reasons. Shelters are frequently full, and she said it was almost impossible to find anywhere else to live. I made calls, stayed on the phone for ninety minutes, and held the line to finally get her what she deserved and was entitled to: a safe and decent place. I then phoned her, gave her the good news, drove her to where she needed to be, bought her and the kids some food, and then began my journey home, hoping this was the end of the day. Then I felt guilty because I was supposed to be on call. "For I was hungry and you gave me food, I was thirsty and you gave me something to drink, I was a stranger and you welcomed me, I was naked and you gave me clothing, I was sick and you took care of me."

There was death and its proximity, as well. I'd visit people in hospital who were dying and accompany priests to people's deathbeds. I'd seen death only when it concerned my loved ones, and never with such regularity. Always remember, I was told, each one is a soul. That was such a crucial piece of advice. Whatever their condition, they are equal in the eyes of God. Never forget, whoever it is, and whether they are young and healthy or old and sick, that the closest we will ever be to God is when we stand facing one of his creations made in his image. There was laughter and there were tears.

I went to visit a woman in hospital who had asked to speak to someone from the church. It was a deeply personal and beautiful time, and perhaps I even managed to do some good. As I left, the man in the next room, whom I'd never met, saw me and shouted that I'd stolen his sausages. He even tried to get out of bed to fight me. He was very old, and I didn't think physical confrontation was likely. It soon became obvious that he wasn't wearing his pyjama trousers, so I was confronted with a very unfortunate man, half-naked, insisting that I'd taken his food. Seminary doesn't really prepare you for such events, so I was very grateful when a nurse suddenly appeared, calmed him, and said to me, "Was it the sausages?" I said yes, it was. "You were lucky," she said. "Last week, he tried to throw a full bedpan at a rabbi over some stolen cheese!"

There was another elderly lady who saw me and said, "I know you. You used to be Michael Coren. I used to like you. Whatever happened to you?"

A very good question.

Or the man who was convinced that I was his son, and when I finally left, he said, "I always preferred your sister, anyway, so you can bugger off."

The reality of what I was training to do and to be. *Is this really what you want, Michael? Oh yes, oh yes, it is.*

Returning to Trinity for studies was a jarring experience because I'd convinced myself that it all seemed so real and gritty out there. What I didn't appreciate was that most of my teachers had been there, done that, far more often than I had. Formation requires learning why and how we're called to do what we do, and that balance between the practical and the intellectual should never be underestimated. There were long — sometimes very long — essays to be written about obscure aspects of the Old Testament, book after book to read about New Testament theory, and courses and lectures involving systematic theology and patristics; if you don't know what they are, look it up. I had the advantage of having been taught Biblical Hebrew as a child, when my father sent me to classes on Sunday mornings. The plan was for me to have a bar mitzvah, although I hardly qualified. Even when I was seven and eight years old, I rebelled against authority, and resented having to go to school outside of weekdays. I moaned and complained and eventually my dad relented and said I didn't have to go anymore. Luckily for me, the Hebrew stuck, and my time in Israel in a period where very few people spoke English expanded my vocabulary. Easy to look clever when you can drop in a sentence or two from an original Biblical language.

I took summer courses, too, because I was determined to complete the M.Div. in three years. Not all the classes were right for me, and I abandoned one of them when the young teacher brought his dog to the class. One of the students had the same idea and the two pups played with each other, in every sense. I love dogs and have always had them as pets, but this didn't exactly add to the harmony of the class. "Ah," said the teacher, "I thought that this might happen." Then why had he brought his dog to the class in the first place? The preparation reading notes he'd given us weren't the right ones; he'd booked the wrong room, so we were squeezed into what was a large cupboard on a very hot day; it was anarchic and politically clumsy; and I didn't return after lunch.

That wasn't a Trinity class and was unusually bizarre. In most of my courses, I was taught about the unbreakable link between Christ, the early church, and the Christianity we have today. We were encouraged to discuss and even disagree, the lecturers were usually eager to help us, and prayer was almost always at the foundation of all that we did. We were given individual spiritual counsellors, which was helpful, listened to guest lecturers, and were allowed to take a certain number of courses at other colleges within the Toronto School of Theology. In addition to Trinity and Wycliffe, I took a course at the Jesuit college, Regis, on spirituality and psychotherapy, and what I learned then has helped me in my daily work as a cleric.

There were regular and frequent interviews with priests and laypeople where we were tested and questioned, and we had to be approved each time before we could progress. The interviewers took their work seriously, read the essays we had to write before each one, and I found it helpful to have to repeatedly articulate why I wanted to be ordained. What fascinated me was that my responses developed each time I was asked. I was learning more than I thought.

□

The work wasn't becoming easier, but it was more negotiable. The finishing line was now a challenge instead of a dream. Nevertheless, some people dropped out of the course, and I understand why. Vocational study isn't the same as a purely academic course; every subject and class was intended to be a means to an end, to prepare us for an entirely new way of living. That can be an enormous burden. One of my difficulties was that I was still working as a journalist, partly because I still had to earn money but also because I always intended to be what is known as "bi-vocational" — not as sexy as it sounds — and maintain part of my media work while, if successful, working as a priest. I'd always seen the areas as symbiotic, and I'm very fortunate that my bishop and those around me agree. There were times when I'd record a radio panel in the morning and then rush off to catch my first lecture of the day or write a newspaper column over lunch and then complete an essay on a fourth-century Church Father in the afternoon.

I was writing quite regularly in Britain now and had been asked to appear on some British news shows. On one vacation in the U.K., I was asked to be a guest on a television show called *Calvin's Common Sense Crusade*, on the GB News network. The show itself would later be cancelled and the host dismissed, and I'm not at all surprised. I've been involved in television for forty years, during which I hosted a daily show for seventeen years and have appeared on Al Jazeera, Fox News, Russia Today, and pretty much everything in between. On this particular show, I was outnumbered two to one — which was fine, if not perfect — and I argued the case for bubble zones around abortion clinics, because a woman had been arrested in England for breaking the law and praying inside the restricted area. I said that women have a right to access medical services without harassment, and that even prayer in close proximity was a form of intimidation. I was asked how, as a Christian, I could justify this. I said that if anything, it was "sinful" to deny women choice, and that the Old Testament even calls for abortion in one case. It was fairly heated, but my main point was that we could compromise: allow prayer but keep it outside of the bubble zone. We can pray anywhere if we genuinely believe in the power of prayer, and must remember that in North America, there's been deadly violence against abortion providers, and clinics have been attacked.

An hour or two later, I looked at Twitter. The host — the eponymous Calvin Robinson — had Tweeted to his 232,000 followers that "for a Christian to be pro-abortion and anti-prayer is bad enough" but for me it was "unfathomable." And "Twisting Scripture like that is wicked … judgment awaits. I pray he repents."

The reaction was predictable. For forty-eight hours, I was flooded with hatred, threats, and abuse. I was used to this sort of thing by now, but it still shocked me that someone could do such a thing, especially when they enjoyed such a large platform. I'm not pro-abortion, would like abortion rates to drop, but believe in women's choice. As for prayer, I'm rather a fan. I'd thought and hoped that this sort of abuse would come to an end but it never has, and whenever I see friends in media suffering under a similar siege, I always reassure them that these campaigns can be tolerated, don't make any lasting difference, and that as the intention is to make people leave various social media platforms, it's important to stay around just so they don't win. Just ignore them — they hate that.

◻

I was working on another book. Dundurn Press in Toronto had approached me and asked if I'd be interested in writing a defence of progressive Christianity. I thought I was too busy to write another book, but this was an offer I couldn't turn down. It would be called *The Rebel Christ*, was published in 2021, and I'm very proud of it. While I was writing it, I sent some passages about 2SLGBTQI+ equality to the actor, author, and thinker Stephen Fry, after a mutual friend gave me his email. I never expected to hear back so was genuinely surprised to receive a personal, effusive, and affectionate response from this world-famous entertainer, wit, and, of course, atheist. I replied, he wrote back, and a friendship began that has been an incalculable joy. He would comment about my writing,

"I live on the other side of the faith debate from Michael, but that doesn't prevent intense admiration of his insight, clarity, courage, and honesty. Integrity, wit and passion. A fine advocate for the best of Christian thought and a faith that encompasses the human as well as the divine." The day I was ordained, he sent an email saying that he was delighted. People can disagree about deeply important issues and still love one another. In fact, it's crucial that they do, if we're ever to make any progress.

□

The third and final year of my masters of divinity arrived — the time when we found out whether ordination was going to happen. I'd passed all the interviews, satisfied the supervisors, had most of my academic credits, and was confident of getting the rest, but there were more hurdles to come. We had to undergo a day-long psychological evaluation, as well as a weekend meeting at a retreat centre where potential clerics gathered for long, extended interviews and to be "observed" by the clergy who were there with us.

The psychological evaluation was at the Southdown Institute, where "preventive and restorative care" is offered to clergy. I was met by someone who was cool bordering on rude. I was early, so had been walking around outside in the snowy countryside. I was told in less than friendly terms to sit in a waiting room. I wondered if this was part of the exam and imagined people watching me through a one-way mirror to see how I reacted to being treated this way.

Then the man who had ordered me about opened the door with a smile and said, "I'm so sorry. Some of our people saw you outside, recognized you as a journalist, and were concerned you'd come to write a story." This was a place mainly for Roman Catholic priests who were residents for various reasons, and the suspicion was entirely understandable. There had been media intrusions in the past.

I was invited into a much more comfortable room, and an hour later, the day of questions and answers began. I passed but what surprised me was the accuracy of the assessment, both the positive and the negative. What I remember about Southdown itself was how much pain was evident in the faces of those who were staying there. We didn't ask them about their history — I don't think we were allowed to, and that was for the best.

The weekend course was at the convent and guesthouse of the Sisterhood of St. John the Divine in Toronto, known as ACPO, the Advisory Committee on Postulants for Ordination. This was a discernment process where we'd all be questioned and examined, and then a report would be sent to our various bishops. Did we have a genuine vocation, did those who monitored us think we were suitable for ordination, and what were our strengths and weaknesses? In other words, it mattered. A bishop didn't have to accept a recommendation or could accept a candidate even if they were turned down, but it was uncommon. That put a lot of pressure on the candidates, and it showed. I found the whole thing quite enjoyable, which I think annoyed some of the dozen other candidates. There seemed to be priests and organizers everywhere, taking it seriously and professionally.

The interviews were long and intense, but I found the questions informed and helpful, and at no time did I feel that anybody was trying to catch me out. I was interviewed by three people together, and then by each of them separately. We were told that the only time we wouldn't be watched was when we were at the Sunday chapel service. Being a natural cynic, I assumed this would be precisely the time we were most watched, so acted accordingly.

There was drama one night, sadly after I'd gone to bed early, when one of the candidates apparently threw a crucifix during a service. Stories do tend to magnify, especially among nervous ordination candidates, and by the time I heard it, the person in question had thrown the cross at the chaplain, the supervisors had met in the middle of the night, and the candidate had been suspended. Whether it all happened like that, I don't know, but the next morning, there were meetings of lugubrious would-be priests and lots of pained, concerned stares. God forgive me but I found it all quite hilarious.

On the final day, we all gathered in a large room and were told that our names would be called out one by one. The candidate would then enter a small room to be told whether they'd be recommended. At that point they'd leave, go back to the large room and, of course, be interrogated by the rest.

Most got through but those who didn't were in understandably bad shape, or sometimes left the building without rejoining us.

My name was called. I sat in front of the three people who had interviewed me. They were unsmiling. *Don't worry, Michael*, I thought, *this is probably standard*. They said they would read out the letter to be sent to my bishop, and that I wasn't to dispute the findings. The letter was quite long but the first or second paragraph said that I was recommended to be ordained. I stopped them, said I needed to take a breath before they continued, and then they all smiled.

At the end of the letter, I hugged all three, left the room, returned to the hall, told my fellow candidates, and then felt a wave of emotion that I hadn't fully anticipated. There had been so much work, so much worry and pressure, and now it appeared it was here. I didn't read the letter properly until later and am so grateful at how enthusiastic my interviewers had been about me. I truly hope I've never let them down.

The week after this was for writing a few final papers and making last preparations for what was to come. I was now on the final stretch. That didn't stop a conservative activist writing to my bishop to question my ordination, or various ugly comments about me on the internet from those who disagreed with my opinions. There was even a downright lie about me that is still sometimes resurrected by people whose mind I seem to occupy to an unhealthy degree. It doesn't allege anything criminal but attacks my character and integrity and is such a grim and cruel distortion. But in such cases, it's best not to respond. Don't get into the mud because you'll never get clean. I pray for the people involved and honestly do forgive them. What mattered more were my own inner demons pinching me with insecurities and doubts. I've never regarded that as a bad thing, as overconfidence for someone in the Christian life can be a horror.

It all seemed to be falling into place, and what I'd been waiting for so long to happen, what I'd worked so hard to make real, was approaching. I was in such a different place, I was such a different me, from a decade earlier.

Ordination was to be Sunday, October 21, 2019. There was no going back. I'd felt this pull for too long for that to happen. The small group of us who were to be ordained went on a retreat, where we prayed, shared, spoke, listened, and worshipped.

The night before my ordination, I knelt in front of the crucifix in my study at home, with a single candle illuminating it in the otherwise darkened room. When I could kneel no longer, I sat, reciting prayers, reading my prayer book and Bible, and asking, asking, asking for help in what was to come. I must have been there for several hours because I woke up the next morning sitting in the same chair, the candle having burned out some time before — I know, it's not wise to fall asleep, leaving a burning candle. I hadn't had much rest, but I felt so alive, so full of enthusiasm and energy. If there had been any reservations, they had disappeared with the flame of that candle.

The day arrived that was to change my life forever. In Christ's Church Cathedral in Hamilton, the mother church of the Anglican

Preaching at St. Luke's Anglican church in Burlington.
Actually, it's posed. I'm far more animated than that usually.

diocese of Niagara, Bishop Susan Bell laid hands on me, and through her episcopal authority ordained me into holy orders. I began the day as one thing, ended it as another. I took oaths, made promises, embarked on a new commitment, and completed a story that had formally started in 2016 with my initial training for the priesthood, but had really begun far earlier than that. Years of study, prayer, and work, all directed toward a vocational pinnacle, fulfilled at the altar of a cathedral with my family, friends, and the assembled church watching. The night before had been like all of the Christmas Eves in the world. The day itself I can compare only with my wedding more than thirty-six years ago. Back then we had cake, this time only cookies.

Yet in all seriousness, I fully understand that a number of people reading this book will be skeptical because they doubt or deny God and Christianity. I say I fully understand because I count some of you as my dearest friends, and to all agnostics and atheists out there, I want to apologize. If Christians had done a better job, if we'd acted more like the founder of our faith had demanded, it would be a hard heart indeed that would take offence.

So, one of my reasons for deciding on this journey, or allowing it to be decided and one I've tried to combine with my media work, is that I want to do all I can to dissolve the indifference or even hostility that so many good and reasonable people have toward organized Christianity.

I'm a deeply flawed, entirely inadequate person to represent Christ, but what I can try to do is attempt to explain him, show him, and then simply not get in the way. Christianity is the permanent revolution of breathtaking and roaring love, an encounter with the rebel Jesus that, in the words of the oath I took that day, calls us "to serve all people, particularly the poor, the weak, the sick, and the lonely."

Ordination is many things, but at its core, it's about practical grace. Feed the hungry, comfort the grieving, support the broken, sit with and listen to the frightened, struggle for the abused and mistreated. Love, peace, and hope. God. Yes, God. God is either everything or nothing, and as I said the words of the oath, I trembled — literally trembled — before the steps of the sanctuary. I know I'm merely one of myriad travellers on the road of faith, pilgrims looking to the shrine of the man who two thousand years ago saw through every lie, every hurt, and every injustice. For this wasn't about me, but something far more significant and timeless.

Sitting in C.S. Lewis's armchair in his study at Magdalene College, Cambridge, in 2023. He's been an influence on me for sixty years.

When I stood with my four fellow deacons, shining new and clearly nervous, and looked into the faces of the congregation, I thought of my parents, who sacrificed so much for me, and of all of those I had lost and am confident I will see once again. Of Dad, who rejected religion but by his love and selflessness reflected God and goodness; of Mum, who raised me in the moral certainty of kindness and care but knew nothing of church. Dad would probably have repeated what he said when I became a Christian. "If it makes you happy, fine. But don't talk to me any more about it." Thing is, I wish I could tell him, and my mum. I wish it very much. May their memory be a blessing. May my memory, please God, eventually be a blessing, too.

"Only in the agony of parting," wrote George Eliot, "do we look into the depths of love." I wasn't sure what was before me, but I knew it would unwind by the day, and that I would meet in the future a pageant still in the making. I knew, I was certain, that each step I now took would not be in isolation. I would not be alone but in the company of those far greater than me. And that gave me more joy than I can ever say.

And so it began. The first time I wore my collar in public, I felt so out of place and out of step. A thin strip of plastic around my neck took on the weight and size of a medieval necklace. I was tempted to take it off on the subway, but I'd made a promise to myself, and to God, to represent Christ and the Church in public and as a journalist. Some people seemed to notice, but most not. Then a young woman approached me and, without introduction or niceties, started to talk about her friend who had just been diagnosed with cancer, how she should react and what she should say to her friend in the weeks and months to come. She asked me if I would pray for her. I said I would.

I haven't stopped praying since.

# ACKNOWLEDGEMENTS

I never thought I'd write a memoir. Then again, I never thought I'd be a priest! There are so many people I need to thank, and for the most part, they won't be listed here — it's just not practical … or at least that's my excuse. To those people I haven't mentioned in the book but who showed me love and help, please forgive me for any oversight. I was given seventy thousand words and God willing, there will be another volume, covering five rather than sixty years, and I can right certain wrongs.

In terms of the book itself, my editor, Russell Smith, has been a joy to work with, and I'll always be grateful to everybody at Dundurn; this is my second, and I hope not my last, book with them. I couldn't ask for a better publisher — and I've worked with quite a number. Special thanks also to Nicholas Freer, who suggested the title, which is far better than the one I originally came up with.

I haven't written very much about my wife and children, partly because I'm not convinced that would be entirely fair, and also because I'm still regularly attacked for my views, and they're sometimes included in those sordid campaigns. I don't want to make their lives any more difficult. But, naturally, I love and thank them.

My oldest friend, Stephen, knows who he is. He has been a rock since I was fourteen years old. It's a privilege to know him.

My journey to an authentic Christian faith and eventually to ordination was the result of so many influences. The writings and friendship of Richard Coles, Mark Oakley, Alan Wilson, Rosie Harper, and Diarmaid MacCulloch, in particular, have been a constant support.

I didn't write this book to score points or to open wounds, and I honestly have tried to be as charitable as possible. Sometimes, however, stinging truths simply can't be avoided. To those who like or even love me, God bless you. To those who dislike or even hate me, God bless you, too.

# ABOUT THE AUTHOR

Michael Coren is a broadcaster, columnist, and speaker. He hosted a daily television show for fifteen years for which he won numerous awards. Michael is a columnist for the *Toronto Star* and a frequent contributor to the *Globe and Mail*, TVO, and the *Walrus* in Canada, and the *New Statesman*, *Times*, *Telegraph*, *Oldie*, and *Church Times* in Britain. He's also a weekly radio broadcaster. He is the bestselling author of eighteen books, including biographies of G.K. Chesterton, H.G. Wells, Arthur Conan Doyle, J.R.R. Tolkien, and C.S. Lewis, and has contributed to the *Dictionary of National Biography* and several other anthologies. Michael has published in many countries and in more than a dozen languages. In 2005, he won the Edward R. Murrow Award for Radio Broadcasting;

in 2006, the RTDNA Canada Radio Broadcasting Award; in 2007, the Communicator Award in Hollywood; and in 2008, the Omni Award for his television show. In 2012, he was awarded the Queen's Jubilee Medal for services to media. Michael is a priest in the Anglican Church of Canada.